THE ROMAN VILLA AT BOX

Mosaic floor in Room 6 as recorded by Sir Harold Brakspear

The Roman Villa at Box

the story of the extensive
Romano-British structures buried below
the village of Box in Wiltshire

MARK CORNEY

commissioned by the KOBRA Trust

on behalf of

**The Box Archaeological
and Natural History Society**

First published in the United Kingdom in 2012
on behalf of the KOBRA Trust
by The Hobnob Press, PO Box 1838, East Knoyle, Salisbury SP3 6FA.
www.hobnobpress.co.uk

British Library Cataloguing in Publication Data
A catalogue record for this book is available from the British Library.

ISBN 978-0-946418-93-0

Typeset in 11/14 pt Chapparal Pro and Zurich Black. Typesetting and origination by John Chandler; jacket design by James Johnson
Printed and bound by CPI Group (UK) Ltd, Croydon, CR0 4YY

Contents

List of Figures

List of Figures

50 Detail of a mosaic from the Chedworth Roman villa showing the personification of Winter gathering sticks for fuel. The figure is wearing a short, hooded cloak known as the Birrus Britannicus

51 Plan of the Colerne villa (After Cosh & Neal, 2005)

52 Location and geophysical survey of the villa south of Euridge Manor Farm (Luckett *et al*, 2000)

53 Engraving by Coles of the Hazelbury Manor mosaic (from Cosh and Neal, 2005, figure 369)

54 Plan of the villa at Atworth (After Erskine and Ellis 2008).

55 Plan of the villa at St Laurence School, Bradford on Avon. Building 1 is the main house; building 2 an agri-industrial structure mimicking the villa house; building 4 includes the bath-suite excavated in 1976. The other buildings are known only from air photography or geophysics and their function remains unknown.

56 Vertical view of the central bi-partite room of the main house at the Bradford on Avon villa showing the well-preserved mosaic floor as exposed in 2003. The circular feature overlying the mosaic floor to the right of centre is thought to be the base of a Christian baptistery dating to the fifth century AD

57 Plan of the Roman roadside settlement at Camerton, north of Radstock. Note the simple plan of the majority of the excavated buildings

58 Plan of the Roman temple and settlement complex on the Fosse Way at Nettleton near Castle Combe. Building 5-6 is the temple, 11-13 the probable guesthouse and 32 a water-mill

59 'Romano-Celtic' stone head from Sunny View Cottage, Henley Lane, Box

60 Replica of a Roman plough

61 Relief from Buzenol in modern Belgium showing a reaping machine called the vallus

62 Part of a mosaic from East Coker in Somerset depicting hunters returning with a deer. A scene such as this will have been common at Box. This floor is now on display in the Somerset County Museum in Taunton

63 A relief depicting a Roman schoolmaster and his pupils. The schoolmaster is seated in the centre with pupils either side; the boy on the far right is arriving late for lessons and no doubt like countless generations since has an implausible excuse ready!

64 A set of Roman bathing equipment from a villa in France. On the left is a pair of bronze instruments called a strigil used for scraping over the body, a bronze vessel for pouring water and, to the right, a glass flask which would have contained scented oil. The bathers at Box would each have owned a set very similar to these

65 An early 5th century AD illustration from a copy of the works of Virgil. The scene is of a formal dinner of the type that will have been held at Box in the 4th century. The diners are reclining on couches and are being served wine by servants. On the table the artist has shown fish and oysters; all foodstuffs that have been recorded from many villas in Roman Britain. The diners are shown with halos; these are originally an artistic device to indicate the rank of the individuals rather than a sign of sanctity

66 Tombstone of the ex-slave woman Regina found at South Shields. She was married to her former master, a man named Barates, probably a military flag

Introduction

DURING 1967 THERE was a routine inspection for a new village hall next to the site of the large Romano-British villa at Box in Wiltshire. This brought professional archaeologists to Box, who eventually managed to extend their investigations beyond the foundation of the new Selwyn Hall. The village of Box and archaeology in general owe a great debt of gratitude to the unknown person responsible for pulling the strings of influence to such good effect.

Inspired by this, a girl and a boy from Box, who were still at school and both budding archaeologists, applied their enthusiasm and remarkable initiative to form the Box Archaeological and Natural History Society (NATS) for short). The father of one of them became treasurer to add gravitas, hardly necessary as most of the initial members were of his generation rather than that of the founders. Sadly one of the founders, Alison Borthwick, died before she could achieve her full potential, but Richard Hodges has been honoured for his services to archaeology and recently appointed president of the American University of Rome.

The new society provided assistance and support for the archaeological campaign at Box, which was now extended to 1968 and 1969. Regrettably publication of the final report had to be delayed for nearly 20 years and by this time local enthusiasm had cooled and the founders were well into their careers. Nevertheless NATS more than justified its existence by organising lectures about and excursions to archaeological and natural history sites.

Then in 2008 the committee of the Society discussed the relative obscurity and ignorance concerning the Roman villa below their village, particularly as it was claimed to be the largest Romano-British complex in the west country second only to the city of Bath itself. It was decided to take action.

A resistivity survey was carried out thanks to the help of Professor Richard Hodges, but this was thwarted by the extensive medieval, modern buildings and debris obscuring the site. The use of underground radar proved to be very expensive as did other non-intrusive methods of investigation. So the Society resorted to concentration on the existing records and reports covering the period from 1828 when the structures were first discovered to the present day and formed the KOBRA Trust (Knowledge Of Box Roman Archaeology) with the following tasks intended to:

> Produce a scholarly Basic Study of the remains for distribution to universities and major archaeological societies.

> Build a model of the ruins for display in the Box library.

> Publish a popular style book for sale at a subsidised price.

> Set up an educational Fund to inform Box school children about their villa.

> Raise funds to finance the first four tasks.

The trustees of the KOBRA Trust are:

> Professor Richard Hodges – chairman of the Trust
> Jenny Hobbs – chairman of NATS.
> Judy Seager – member of Box Parish Council.
> Ronnie Walker – executive trustee.

The trustees have appointed Mark Corney as consulting archaeologist, co-coordinator of the Basic Study and author of this book. Christine Williams of Newton Abbot has made the model. The Rev Canon John Ayers has acted as moderator and Dr John Chandler as editor for this book.

Raising finance proved to be very difficult as neither the Heritage Lottery Fund nor any of the major archaeological societies except the Association for Roman Archaeology were able to assist. Eventually the £18,000 necessary for the Project was contributed by local donations from the residents of Box plus others, anonymous sponsorships and Inland Revenue Gift Aid. The largest contributor was Wiltshire Council, which provided a most welcome £5,000. The Basic Study has now been completed and distributed to university archaeology departments and major archaeology societies. The Model is now on display at Box Library and planning is underway to establish the Educational Fund.

The new alignments reported in this book, which resulted from the Basic Study have proved beyond reasonable doubt that the Romano-British structures at Box are among the largest complexes found to date in the west of England. While the core will probably remain inaccessible for the foreseeable future, there is great potential for peripheral excavation and many secrets to be uncovered such as:

Why is the Hermitage ditch and its valuable pottery at a higher level than the core buildings? Is there an earlier villa yet to be found?

Why have no middens been discovered, the rubbish must be somewhere?

Why have only a small number of coins been found?

Was Box a sacred site?

We who have worked on the KOBRA Project cannot help but wonder who will carry Alison's and Richard's young dream to the maturity of fuller archaeological understanding and add meaningfully to our knowledge of Roman Britain.

Ronnie Walker
Executive Trustee

Author's Preface

THIS BOOK IS the result of an in-depth study of the Roman remains beneath the village of Box. It is aimed at the general reader and has tried to keep technical terms to a minimum. A more detailed archaeological appraisal of the site has been prepared for publication elsewhere and those who wish to know more will find copies of this deposited at the Wiltshire & Swindon History Centre in Chippenham.

Many people have assisted in the writing of the book and their help is gratefully acknowledged here. Especial thanks are due to the staff at the Wiltshire & Swindon History Centre, Devizes Museum, The National Monuments Records Centre, Nicola Morris and Rob Bell.

Special thanks must go to Ronnie Walker, Executive Trustee of the KOBRA Trust, for inviting me to undertake the study of the Box villa and providing constant encouragement throughout the project.

Mark Corney

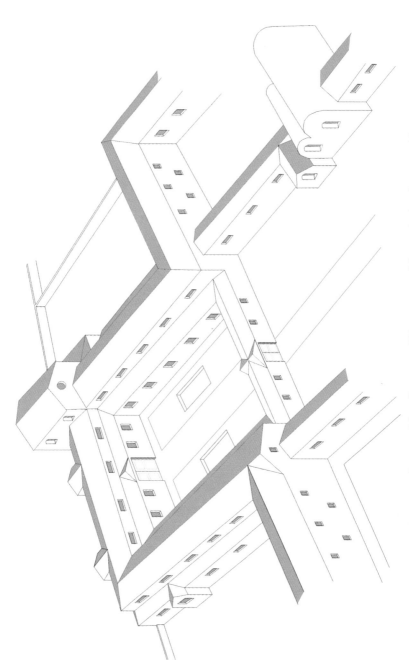

1 *Reconstruction drawing of the villa as it would have appeared during the fourth century AD.*

1

The Discovery
of the Villa at Box

Setting the Scene

THE DRAWING ON the page facing this opening chapter is an artist's impression of the Roman villa at Box as it probably looked sixteen hundred years ago (Figure 1). It had at least 42 rooms, nearly half of which had mosaic floors – some of great beauty. The windows were glazed and a large number of the rooms had under-floor heating. The interior walls of most rooms were plastered and decorated to give the impression of marble, while the outside was dressed stone and plastered rubble with a tiled roof. One luxurious bath suite has been discovered. This is inadequate for the size of the villa and it is highly probable that at least one more bath complex remains to be located.

At least thirty villas have been discovered to date in the neighbourhood of the city of Bath and of these the villa at Box is the largest and best appointed. However the 42 rooms refer only to the excavated parts of the villa. Research during the current study has demonstrated the probability of further extensive structures under the gardens of Box House to the west and beyond the Vicarage to the east. These add significantly to the overall size of the villa as a whole.

The core buildings of the villa are set on a hardened limestone or tufa terrace occupying a gentle north-west facing slope at a height of between 46m and 38m above sea level. The terrace overlooks the valley of the By Brook (or Box Brooke) a tributary of the River Avon. As can be seen from Figure 2 the central buildings consist of a main east-west range on the north edge of the terrace and two north-south ranges forming a courtyard layout. The north range and the northern parts of the two supporting ranges are free of over-build and lie under the garden of 'The Wilderness', which stands on the site of a medieval mill and millrace. This millrace destroyed the southern part of the west range, which probably extended under the churchyard of St Thomas Becket Church. The east range is relatively intact although now overbuilt by two semi-detached houses erected by a late nineteenth century exploiter of the site. While the core buildings are free of overbuild except for the east range, further buildings lie under the Selwyn Hall, the Vicarage, the Church, the Churchyard, Box House Cottage, Box House garden and Box House itself. In addition to the tufa terrace, further terraces are clearly visible in the grounds of The Wilderness; these may be artificial and potentially of Roman date.

The First Discoveries

THE STORY OF investigation at the villa is almost as dramatic as the story of the villa itself. It extends over nearly two hundred years and is a strange mixture of greed and altruism. There has long been a myth among Box folk of a Roman and a pre-Roman presence in their village. According to one of the early letters to the *Gentleman's Magazine* as recently as 1831 or thereabouts a miscreant before the magistrates gave his address as an unknown street he called 'Traut's Lane' – Traut being a supposed pre-Roman god! There were also tales of beautiful mosaics found in the churchyard by the grave diggers. These proved to be true when in 1833 the Rev George Mullins, the vicar of Ditteridge, wrote to the *Gentleman's Magazine* confirming that a few years before a tesselated pavement had been found in the garden of his house 'The Wilderness' while digging foundations. The early Victorians of the second half of the 19th century regarded archaeology very differently from our present day viewpoint. Gentlemen antiquarians, often of independent means and with the benefit of a classical education, would indulge in excavation to expose Roman remains but archaeology as the discipline we know it today had yet to develop. There were also entrepreneurs for whom archaeological remains and artefacts had a commercial potential. It is against this background that we should judge the investigations of Mr Mullins and his successors.

Excavations were on a major scale on what is now known as the north range of the villa. North from the pavement first discovered by Mullins, he tells of traces of another pavement found 43 yards distant, but largely destroyed. Between them were seven stone pillars of rough workmanship; and nearby was what is described as an altar-like erection consisting of several stones, and a piece of stone of a semicircular shape, about 1 foot across, and 8 inches thick, partially excavated on each side, as if for holding something. This stone bore marks of fire. Some 28 yards to the west were the mutilated

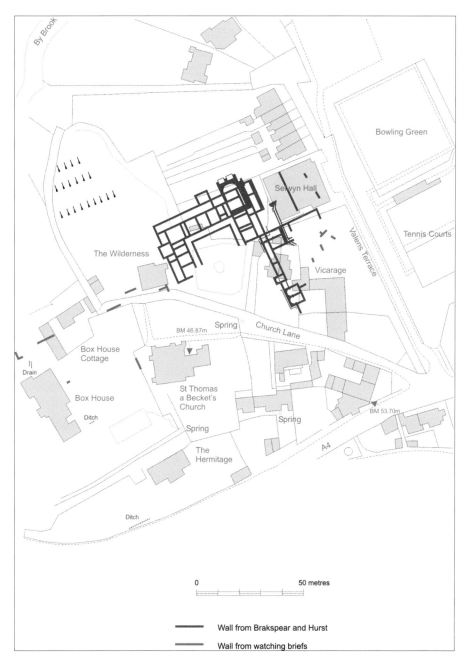

2 Plan of the known remains of the Box Roman villa and modern features

remains of yet a further tessellated pavement of blue stones, ornamented with two red borders; the tesserae being nearly 1 inch square, and the blue stones entirely decomposed. This pavement, in its original state, must have been at least 10 or 12 feet square. The remains of a wall on the south side contained several flues made of whole bricks supported by iron cramps; and underneath the bed on which the pavement was laid, made of a coarse gravel and mortar, were large flags supported by pillars of stone forming a regular hypocaust.

An opening in the direction of the hypocaust and at a depth of 4 feet yet another tessellated pavement was discovered, very nearly perfect and apparently forming a passage from some other part of the building. This pavement is 9 feet wide, 28 feet long, and turns at a right angle 6 feet from where it is broken up; but it evidently extended much further in both directions. The pattern of this passage is particularly elegant. The ground-colour is white; the exterior tesserae coarse; two blue lines of small cubes form the border, 6 feet apart; and the intermediate space is filled with semicircles forming waving lines, blue, crossing each other at right angles. These are again intersected by others of half the diameter, with their extremities united in the middle, and terminating in small crosses shaded with red and yellow, white and blue, and producing a most beautiful effect. In one corner a curious stone was found shaped like a seat, but only 8 inches high. Several specimens of painted plaster from the walls were recovered. They were coloured very brightly when first exposed to the air. The patterns were principally imitations of marble panels, with elegant coloured bordering; but none bore any representation of figures. A small vase, holding about a pint and described as being apparently of British workmanship, was dug up near the pillars, but unfortunately damaged. One room was paved with plain square red bricks. Only one small coin was found but so corroded as to be wholly illegible.

Mr Mullins reported another piece of pavement which he had not yet seen in a distant part of his garden and concluded that the whole of the original buildings, if square, must have covered a considerable portion of ground, the most distant of the pavements being at least 50 yards apart.

It seems that during the next 25 years, the garden of the Wilderness and surrounding areas was subdivided into 5 plots (Fig. 3, A to E). Sufficient excavation took place to justify an auction sale in 1855 of mosaics in plot A which was attended by a Mrs Casenove, who was so impressed with the beauty of one mosaic that she made a tracing of it on copies of spare bills of sale.

Despite commercial interest there were a few concerned voices crying in the wilderness. In 1860 Mr H Syer Cuming wrote a letter to the *Journal of the British Archaeological Association* quoting a friend who lived at the site

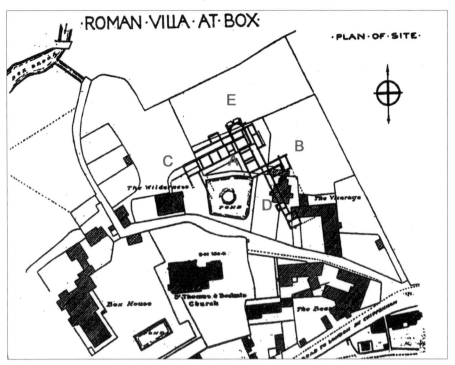

3 The Wilderness Garden and surrounding areas subdivided as Areas A-E

of the Box Roman ruins and who encouraged the removal of the Roman broken bricks, tiles, tessellated pavement, etc. from his garden. The account described the exposure of the East Baths of the villa, noted as being 'quite perfect', and gave a description of the patterns on box-flue tiles. Mr Cuming's communication to the British Archaeological Association was prompted by his concern that the remains were being removed for use as road mending material. He writes, 'if those details be not collected speedily, we shall have to search and ransack the highways and byways for what once constituted the well appointed dwelling of some opulent Roman family seeking health and recreation in the region of the ancient Belgae.'

Twenty years later someone with a very different attitude to Mr Cuming took the stage. At some time during or prior to 1879 a Mr Stier, who had a jewellery business at 19 New Bond Street, Bath, acquired plot D which contained the bath suite reported by Mr Mann (Figure 4). Mann had already been closely involved with the early excavations of the Roman Baths in Bath which were opened for public viewing as a commercial venture in 1879.

This perhaps suggested to Mr Stier that mosaics and other artefacts

4 *View of the East Baths as excavated. Although undated, this photograph must have been taken at the time of its discovery in 1881 and prior to removal for public exhibition in London*

from Box could also be displayed or sold commercially. By 1888 a mosaic floor from the Box villa, discovered in 1881, is known to have been on public display in London (Figure 5).

Mr Mann's paper in 1886 states that, 'The plot of ground on which this portion of the villa stands was put up for sale by auction by the owners: but failing to sell they subsequently removed the semicircular bath, fixing it in a framework of wood and iron to allow for its transportation from place to place for exhibition. The tesselae (*sic*), which were used by the Romans with their natural cleavage faces, have now been polished, resulting in giving a colour and appearance akin to ivory. As to the site of this portion of the villa, the ground has been levelled and a house built upon it (subsequently two semi-detached dwellings named 'Roman Villas 1 and 2') – a result much to be regretted. Thus are such priceless relics lost.'

Presumably having made a profit Mr Stier disappeared from the scene and nothing further happened for a decade. The fate of the removed bath and mosaic is unknown.

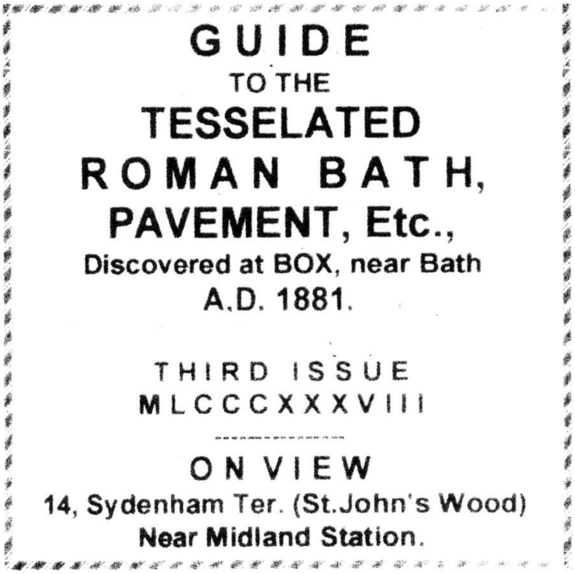

GUIDE
TO THE
TESSELATED
ROMAN BATH,
PAVEMENT, Etc.,
Discovered at BOX, near Bath
A.D. 1881.

THIRD ISSUE
MLCCCXXXVIII

ON VIEW
14, Sydenham Ter. (St.John's Wood)
Near Midland Station.

5 *Flyer for the public exhibition of Roman remains from Box (the
date in Roman numerals must be a misprint and presumably
should have read MDCCCLXXXVIII)*

Mr Hardy and Sir Harold Brakspear

IN 1897 MR John Hardy of Box, who had inherited the family business of
a general store, purchased the land to the north of plot D where Stier had
excavated the Roman baths and mosaics. A plan showing the area purchased
survives (Figure 6) showing in blue the extent of Hardy's acquisition of Plots
A and E.

At this distance Mr Hardy is something of an enigma. There is no doubt
that he was an enthusiastic amateur archaeologist, but he may also have had
an eye on the commercial potential of the site. There are still whispers of a
rumour in the village that Mr Hardy let it be thought he had bought the land
to grow vegetables for his shop.

In the event Mr Hardy excavated in Plot A during 1897 and 1898 and
left the excavations open over the winter causing frost damage to exposed
mosaics. As a consequence of this damage the excavations were backfilled in
1898. For a further four years nothing was done and then in 1902 Mr Hardy
persuaded or arranged with Mr W Heward Bell of Seend, near Devizes, to
finance further investigations in 1902 and 1903. The circumstance of this
association is unknown. Mr W Heward Bell had made a considerable fortune
from Welsh coal and was an eccentric character known as 'Squire Bell.' He

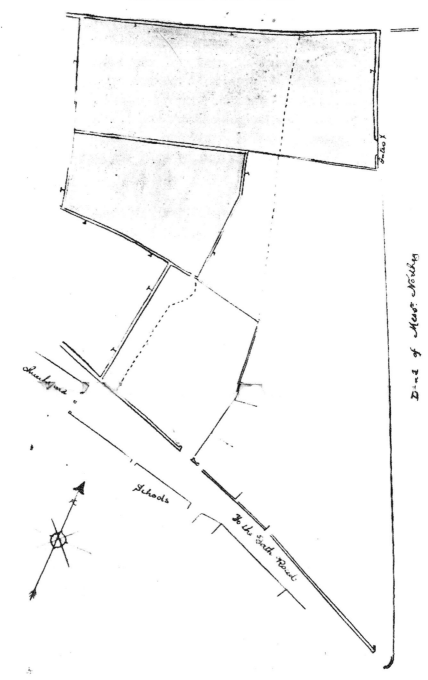

6 Plan showing in blue the land acquired to the north of Plot D by Hardy in 1897

was father to Clive Bell, a member of the Bloomsbury Group in London. Mr
Heward Bell financed the cost of the investigations and is thought to have

employed Mr Harold (later Sir Harold) Brakspear to record the excavations and prepare a report, although Brakspear gives the impression of working for the Wiltshire Archaeological and Natural History Society. Brakspear was a leading archaeologist of this period with a keen interest in medieval architecture.

Whatever the details, the partnership of Hardy, Heward Bell and Brakspear provided the core of our knowledge about Romano-British Box and their work has formed the basis for all subsequent investigations. The report on the excavations was published by Brakspear in the *Wiltshire Archaeological Magazine* in 1904. As is usual for many nineteenth and early twentieth century excavations, little account was made of the archaeological stratigraphy (this being the successive layers which form on archaeological sites whose recording forms the basis of detailed study) and it is probable that the remains were uncovered using largely unskilled labour with little supervision. As a consequence much important evidence, especially that relating to the decline and abandonment of the villa, would have been lost. In spite of the extent of Hardy's excavations relatively few finds were recorded.

Modern Archaeological Investigation Commences

NO FURTHER WORK on the complex was undertaken until 1967-8 when Henry Hurst excavated the area now occupied by the Selwyn Hall and immediately to the east of the villa remains dug by Hardy. The work on the site of the Selwyn Hall recorded further walls, drains or culverts and recovered the first stratified groups of finds. Hurst also re-excavated the north-east corner of the villa and examined the large chamber room 26 with a rounded end or apse. The re-excavation of room 26 demonstrated the complexity of the building sequence and Hurst was able to identify at least four major phases spanning the second to fourth centuries AD (Figure 7). Relatively little material was recovered from the 1967-8 excavations, especially of pottery which is normally so prolific on Roman sites. This would suggest that the lack of finds from Hardy's work may not be merely the result of the poor standards of excavation. Hurst's report was published in the *Wiltshire Archaeological Magazine* for 1987.

Since the 1967-8 work there has been no further investigation of the main villa buildings although small-scale observations and excavations close by have produced interesting, if sometimes fragmentary, results.

In 1982, Mrs Kate Carless, then owner of The Wilderness, excavated a

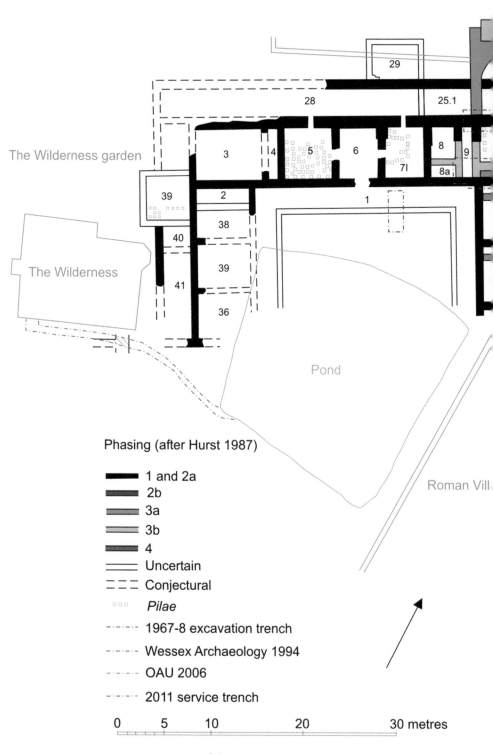

The Wilderness garden

The Wilderness

29

28

25.1

3

4

5

6

8

9

7l

8a

2

1

39

38

40

39

41

36

Pond

Roman Vill

Phasing (after Hurst 1987)

1 and 2a
2b
3a
3b
4
Uncertain
Conjectural
Pilae
1967-8 excavation trench
Wessex Archaeology 1994
OAU 2006
2011 service trench

0   5   10   20   30 metres

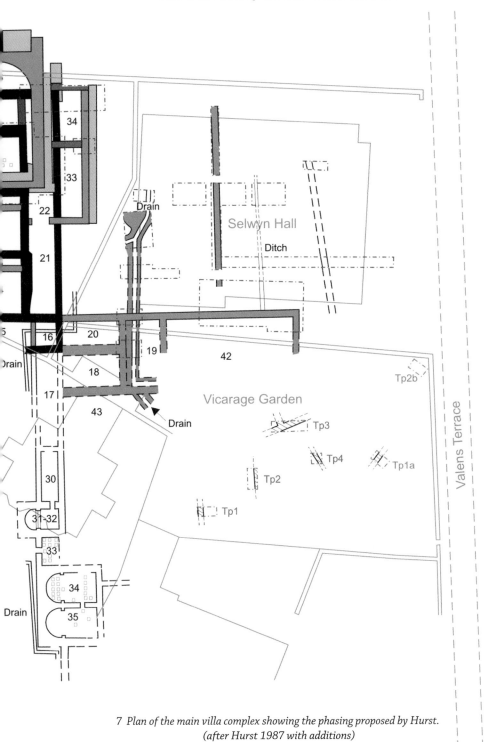

7 Plan of the main villa complex showing the phasing proposed by Hurst.
(after Hurst 1987 with additions)

7 metre length of a Roman ditch discovered in the grounds of The Hermitage 100 metres south of the main villa. The ditch is described as being aligned east-west and 'shallow 'V' shaped'. The ditch produced the largest stratified group of Roman pottery yet known from Box (weighing 49.2 kilos) and other materials, including vessel and window glass, metalwork, and 18 kilos of Roman brick and tile. The most notable find was a silver plaque in the form of a life-size human eye, possibly intended to be a religious offering to a healing cult like that of the goddess Sulis-Minerva at Bath. The pottery from The Hermitage ditch is of considerable importance as it includes first and second century AD material and probably pre-dates the construction of the first villa buildings. The glass included a colourless ring with a yellow surface decoration which may be pre-Roman in date, possibly of the 2nd or 1st century BC. The Hermitage ditch points to a major focus of early Roman activity south of the later villa site and suggests a substantial building nearby which still awaits discovery.

Since 1982 work on the site has been largely restricted to small-scale archaeological watching briefs and evaluations associated with building development works and services, as required under the Archaeological Areas Act passed in 1979. These informative observations have produced significant new information on the extent of the site, especially to the west of the villa in the area of Box House Cottage and Box House. Since 1982 work has been undertaken by four separate commercial archaeological units and remarkably none of these observations has been combined to produce a detailed overall plan until now (Figure 7).

Very little of the villa is visible today. Of the areas examined by Hardy only a small portion of wall is visible in the grounds of The Wilderness. This is private property and not accessible. Part of the boundary wall between Box House and the churchyard is seated on part of an earlier wall, 5 metres long and with all the appearance of being Roman. The wall stands up to three courses high; it is wider than the rest of the boundary wall and is on the north-south axis of the villa. It is quite possible that this is a surviving piece of Roman masonry (Figure 8: I am very grateful to Mr Rob Bell of Box for pointing this out).

Since the initial correspondence in the *Gentleman's Magazine* in the 1830s describing the discovery of Roman remains, investigations in and around The Wilderness and adjoining properties have established the presence of a major Roman building of considerable scale and wealth. This has been called a 'Roman villa' implying that it was the home of a rich landowning family. This may indeed be part of the story although the fragmentary and as

8 View of the boundary wall between Box House and the churchyard showing three courses of possible Roman masonry in situ at the base of the wall

yet poorly understood remains extending into Box House and the grounds of the Vicarage clearly indicate a more extensive complex.

In the following chapters the development of the region as part of the Roman empire will be examined and the role and function of the Box villa will be examined.

2

Setting the Scene and the Coming of Rome

Before the Romans

THERE ARE FEW places in southern Britain without evidence of early human activity. Box is no exception. The earliest artefacts are worked flint tools dating from the Mesolithic period, between 10,000BC and 4,000BC, which mark the passage of nomadic hunters and gatherers following the end of the last Ice Age. Over the next 3,000 years the farming of domesticated animals and crops developed and the use of flint for tools and weapons gave way first to bronze and then iron. By the Iron Age, generally agreed to begin about 750-700BC, much of the country was divided up into fields with a dense pattern of settlements. On Bathampton Down south of Bath, on Charmy Down to the north of Bath and in Inwood, south of Kingsdown, there are extensive remains of Iron Age fields and settlements which survive as well preserved earthworks (Figure 9). Once established, many of the fields remained in use throughout the Roman period and in some areas still influence the layout of the modern landscape.

The Roman landscape of the Box region has its origins in the Iron Age and it, along with the people and politics of this period, need to be described before we examine the impact of the arrival of Rome.

For much of the Iron Age the most highly visible settlements which survive in the modern landscape are hillforts. With origins between 1,000BC and 700BC, these monuments represent a major investment in manpower and community resources, and probably mark a growing cohesion of scattered agricultural communities. The function of hillforts is complex and changed during the passage of the first millennium BC. It is thought that the earliest hillforts were centres for special gatherings, the corralling of livestock and

9 Air photograph of Bathampton Down showing the clear remains of prehistoric field boundaries, a large hillfort and settlements all underlying the modern golf course

the storage of surplus produce to be used in exchange for exotic commodities. In the Box area hillforts are known on Bathampton Down, Bradford on Avon, Little Solsbury Hill and at Bury Wood, Colerne. The Bathampton Down site is a fine example of an early Iron Age hillfort (Figure 9). At Bradford on Avon is Budbury hillfort, now largely destroyed, where excavation demonstrated that the fort was constructed about 700BC and abandoned about 300BC. The hillfort on Little Solsbury Hill is probably of similar date to Budbury.

Between 400BC and 300BC certain hillforts were abandoned whilst others continued to be occupied. Of those which continued in use the defences were frequently increased in scale and the entrances became more complex. These are known as developed hillforts and there is evidence for permanent settlement within them with substantial roundhouses, industrial activities and provision for the processing and storage of agricultural produce. The hillforts now became important regional centres and will have provided a range of services and support for the surrounding agricultural communities. The hillfort of Bury Wood Camp in Colerne parish, ten kilometres to the north of Box, is the nearest example of a developed hillfort. Excavations here between 1959 and 1966 showed that occupation commenced by 600BC with major modifications occurring during the fourth century BC and, from this period, it contained roundhouses and evidence for iron working and agricultural processing. The site continued in use into the first century BC when, in common with many other hillforts in southern Britain, it was abandoned.

Although they survive in large numbers, hillforts are only one component of a very diverse range of Iron Age settlements. The majority of the pre-Roman population living in farming settlements were probably based upon the extended family unit. Many of the settlements were enclosed by a bank and ditch and set within an ordered landscape of fields and tracks.

10 Air photograph of an Iron Age type settlement south of Malmesbury

The bank and ditch around each settlement was probably not for defence but rather served as a boundary and to prevent animals from straying. In west Wiltshire and the eastern side of the Cotswold Hills these enclosed settlements tend to be of rectilinear plan (Figure 10). An enclosure of possible Iron Age date has been recorded by air photography at Hazelbury Manor, 2km to the south-east of Box, and close to the site of a possible Roman villa. Where such sites have been excavated they typically have two or three roundhouses, constructed either in dry stone or timber (Figure 11), have pits used as underground storage silos, hearths, ovens, stock compounds and, occasionally, evidence for the working of iron and bronze. Finds include large amounts of pottery, mostly local in origin and handmade although some exotic products do occur, bone and metal tools and large quantities of animal bone representing the main Iron Age domesticated species of cattle, sheep and pig. On what are sometimes interpreted as 'high status' or more specialised sites horse may also be present. Surprisingly, wild animals such as boar and deer are relatively rare although antler was used for the manufacture of tools and handles. From the beginning of the first century AD some settlements in the region showed signs of growing wealth and were able to access fine imported pottery and metalwork manufactured in the Roman world and traded into Britain via a series of harbours along the south coast. Air photography has revealed a number of probable Iron Age farms to the north and south of Box.

By the last half of the first century BC, soon after the abandonment of many hillforts, distinctive regional distribution patterns of pottery styles, metalwork and coins become increasingly apparent. These patterns, also often associated with new types of settlements known as *oppida* (a Latin term for a town), are generally accepted as evidence for the emergence of tribal societies, although we know little about how they were organised. We know that after the Roman conquest of AD43 the new province of Britannia was governed on tribal districts and these are presumed to be largely based on pre-conquest groupings. It is from the Roman period that we have the names of the tribes and can only assume them to have been the same, or similar, name during the late Iron Age. Subtle variations in the regional artefact types suggest that many of the 'tribes' attested after the Roman conquest may in fact have been confederations of more independent groupings and there may even have been aristocratic immigrants from Gaul, modern France, settling in the region. In western Britain the Cotswold Hills, lower Severn Valley and surrounding areas are usually identified as being the territory of a tribe known as the *Dobunni* during the Roman period.

11 Reconstruction of an Iron Age roundhouse at Castell Henllys, Wales

Coinage, ascribed to the *Dobunni* and initially only struck in gold and of a standard weight, began to circulate in the Cotswolds, the lower Severn Valley, the northern part of Somerset and west Wiltshire before the end of the first century BC. The coins bear legends, in Latin, giving personal names such as *Comux* and *Catti*. Early in the first century AD silver coins began to circulate alongside gold issues and further names appear; *Anted, Eisu, Corio* and *Bodvoc* (Figure 12).

In the past these named coins have been interpreted as representing 'kings', and complex pseudo-historical dynastic sequences have been proposed. Current opinion is more reserved, and the significance of the names may be more complex although some may be of rulers. The distribution of the coins suggests that there may have been a number of mint sites operating at any one time. Debris from the minting of coins in the form of moulds for casting blank pellets have been excavated at Bagendon and The

12 Gold coin of 'Anted' (left) and a silver coin of 'Bodvoc' (right)

Ditches, North Cerney, both to the north of Cirencester. Other locations doubtless await discovery. Whatever the true significance of these coins may be, the use of standard weights suggests a series of linked centralised fiscal authorities responsible for their minting and distribution. At the same time as the coins appear in the archaeological record new types of settlements began to appear. These are characterised by large tracts of land partially enclosed by extensive and complex systems of ditches and banks. Known as *oppida* to archaeologists, these sites first appeared in south-eastern Britain during the mid-first century BC and within fifty years the tradition had spread into parts of western Britain. Within the area of Dobunnic coin distribution a number of these sites are known, notably at Bagendon near Cirencester and

on Minchinhampton Common near Stroud. Other possible examples are hinted at by concentrations of coins and other finds of late Iron Age metalwork at Camerton to the south of Bath and Mells near Frome (Figure 14). A further late Iron Age centre may be suspected at Bath. Here, there are finds of Iron Age coins from the sacred spring within the later Roman temple complex and a late Iron Age settlement of unknown extent has been partially investigated at Lower Common to the west of the later Roman town.

The major late Iron Age centres in the region were linked into an extensive trade and exchange network with connections to south-east Britain and across the English Channel to Roman Gaul, modern France. Via these routes numerous luxury items originating in the Roman world entered Britain. Amongst the commodities imported were amphorae (large ceramic vessels) containing Italian wines and fish sauces from southern Spain (Figure 13); fine table pottery from Gaul and Italy and metalwork.

13 A Roman amphora made in Italy between 50BC and 10BC which originally held 25 litres of top quality wine. These vessels are imported into Britain in large numbers towards the end of the Iron Age

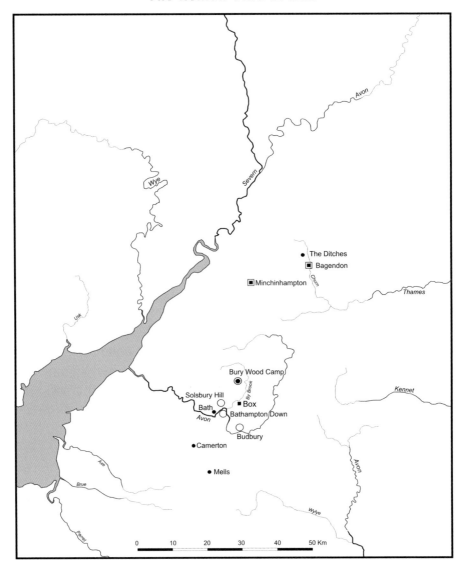

14 Iron Age sites mentioned in the text

The archaeological evidence demonstrates that the main elements of this trade were associated with eating and drinking in a romanised fashion. It is highly probable that Roman provincial merchants were present in Britain from the late first century BC and were engaged in trade with the upper echelons of native British society. The *oppida*, such as Bagendon, played a key role in this trade and the further distribution of Roman imports in western Britain. There can be little doubt that Rome was beginning to have both economic and political influence across southern Britain for at least fifty years before the conquest of AD43. The cross-channel trade links may also be evidence of Roman diplomatic embassies to many of the southern British tribes, including the Dobunni. In this context the use of Latin characters on the late Iron Age coins can be viewed as further evidence of growing Roman political, cultural and economic influence. Some even think that young British aristocrats may have been sent to Rome to receive an education and no doubt develop pro-Roman tendencies. This is certainly a well-attested part of Roman foreign policy during the reign of the emperor Augustus and his successors and may in part account for the widespread use of Latin on native British coinage.

The Arrival of Rome

D IRECT ROMAN MILITARY intervention in Britain began in the mid-first century BC. In 58BC Julius Caesar commenced his conquest of Gaul (modern France and Belgium) and in his account of the campaigns Caesar tells us that the northern Gallic tribes had been receiving military and other aid from Britain. This was used as a pretext to launch an attack on Britain in the late summer of 55BC. Caesar crossed the English Channel with two legions and landed somewhere on the coast of east Kent, probably near Deal. The landing was opposed but eventually a bridgehead was established. It is highly likely that Caesar had underestimated the difficulties of crossing the Channel and establishing a firm foothold in Britain. Hostages were taken but a severe storm threatened the beached fleet and Caesar swiftly retired to Gaul. In the following year, 54BC, he returned. This time he was better prepared. He crossed earlier in the summer and had a much larger force, comprising five legions plus cavalry, possibly as many as 30,000 troops in total. He tells us that he advanced inland, crossed the River Thames and eventually defeated a British force under the command of an elected war leader named Cassivellaunus. The actual site of the battle is unknown but it is thought to have been either in eastern Hertfordshire or western Essex. Following the British surrender further hostages were taken, treaties concluded and diplomatic and economic links established between a number of south-eastern British tribes and Rome. Caesar never returned to Britain and ten years later he was dead and the Roman world plunged into civil war. The victor, Caesar's adopted heir Octavian, triumphed and in 27BC changed his name to Augustus and established the Roman empire, thus marking the end of the Roman republic. It is in this period that we see the large scale importation of wine, pottery, metalwork and other luxury goods.

In AD41 the Roman emperor Gaius (known to history by his nickname Caligula) was murdered and his uncle, Claudius, the last adult male member of the Julio-Claudian family, was proclaimed emperor (Figure 15). Claudius' succession was by no means secure and he needed to consolidate his position as emperor. From the fragmentary surviving contemporary documentary sources it appears that there was political instability in southern Britain following the death of a ruler named Cunobelin. This may have provided a pretext for Claudius to seek military glory by undertaking the conquest of Britain. A successful invasion would provide Claudius with military prestige and establish him as a worthy successor to his illustrious forebears; his grandfather was Mark Antony and his older brother, Germanicus, had been one of the most successful generals under the first emperor Augustus.

In the summer of AD43 a large army was assembled at Boulogne, the main Roman harbour on the Gallic (French) side of the English Channel. Commanded by Aulus Plautius, one of Claudius' leading generals, the force comprised four legions supported by auxiliary regiments. The total number of troops involved must have been in the region of 40,000 men. The legions, the Second Augusta, the Twentieth, the Ninth Hispana and the Fourteenth Gemina had been drawn from frontier bases along the River Rhine and the River

15 Coin of the emperor Claudius showing triumphal arch commemorating the conquest of Britain

Danube. These regiments were highly disciplined heavy infantry, about 5000 strong, all Roman citizens and, at this date, recruited mainly from southern France, northern Italy and Spain. The legions were supported by Auxiliary regiments of about 500 men. These were recruited from the provinces and often provided specialist units such as the Batavians (from the Rhine delta) who could ford and swim rivers in full battle kit or cavalry. The majority of auxiliary troops were not Roman citizens but on completion of 25 years service they received full citizenship. We know from early Roman tombstones found in Britain (including examples from Bath) that auxiliary units raised across the Empire including Spain, France, Germany and the Balkans were present in the invasion force (Figure 16).

Unlike the first invasion led by Julius Caesar 97 years earlier, contemporary accounts record that the landing of Claudius' army was unopposed and a bridgehead rapidly established. In recent years a lively debate has developed over the precise site of the Roman landing with a number of academics challenging the traditional location of Kent in favour of Fishbourne Harbour to the west of Chichester. On balance the Kent location still seems the most likely, this being the shortest direct crossing from the port of embarkation at Boulogne. The main invasion force probably landed at Richborough near modern Sandwich where archaeological investigations have uncovered extensive military remains of this period. Further landings were subsequently made further to the west; early Roman military bases have been excavated at Fishbourne and Chichester in West Sussex and immediately to the north of Poole Harbour at Lake Farm near Wimborne in Dorset (Figure 17).

16 Tombstone of the trooper Genialis found at Cirencester. Genialis served in the Ala Thracorum, a cavalry regiment originally raised in the Balkans

The primary objective of the invading forces was the major tribal centre of *Camulodunum*, modern Colchester. The most powerful tribal confederation in south-eastern Britain, the Catuvellauni, was based here and the site had emerged as an important political and economic centre during the early first century AD. Contemporary sources tell of the invading Roman army having to fight a battle to force the crossing of an unidentified river, crossing the River Thames, then halting to await the arrival of Claudius (accompanied by war elephants) before advancing on to capture Colchester where the Emperor personally received the surrender of a number of British leaders.

In addition to the contemporary literary sources the archaeological evidence is beginning to show a complex series of military events in the first year or so of the conquest with rapid advances across much of southern Britain. Large forts associated with the initial advance westwards and

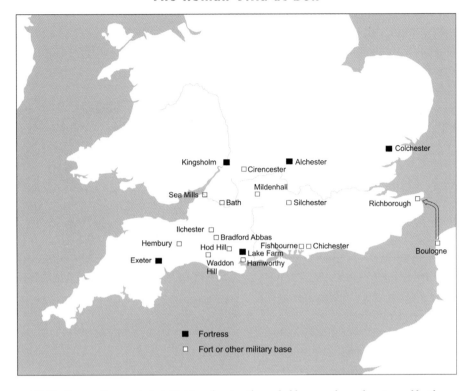

17 The Roman Conquest of AD43. Map showing the probable cross-channel route used by the invading army and the known Roman military sites in western Britain dating to between AD43 and AD55

probably functioning as legionary campaign bases have been identified at Alchester near Oxford and Lake Farm south of Wimborne in Dorset, with further large bases being established at Kingsholm near Gloucester by AD 50 and Exeter by AD 55.

The archaeological evidence for British resistance to the invading forces is varied and highly regional. Roman forts of the conquest period are comparatively rare across much of south-eastern Britain. Further west, especially into Dorset and eastern Devon, there are at least a dozen confirmed forts holding garrisons of between 500 to 1000 troops with a legionary fortress established at Exeter for the Legio II Augusta by the early 50s AD. This legion is known to have been commanded by the future emperor Vespasian during the conquest and his biographer tells us that he captured at least twenty strongholds and the Isle of Wight during the campaign. At Hod Hill hillfort near Blandford Forum excavation has graphically revealed evidence for a Roman assault followed by construction of an earth and timber fort, the remains of which can still be seen (Figure 18). Further evidence for Roman attacks come from Maiden Castle, Pilsdon Pen (both in Dorset), Hembury in east Devon, South Cadbury (and possibly Ham Hill) both in south Somerset. Other sites doubtless await discovery.

In western Britain, around the Upper Thames Valley, Cotswold Hills and the lower Severn Estuary the pattern of early Roman military sites is somewhat different. Here the evidence for resistance is minimal and although a number of forts are known these are mainly at strategic points along the routes which eventually become the main Roman roads in the region. This suggests that there was a less belligerent attitude in the area.

18 *Aerial view of Hod Hill in Dorset with the Roman fort (foreground) constructed within one corner of the Iron Age hillfort*

There is one curious reference by the late second century AD Roman historian Cassius Dio that may refer to an event in the region. Dio writes: 'Plautius [the Roman commander] secured the voluntary alliance of a group of the Bodunni, a people dominated by the princes of the Catuvellauni, namely Caratacus and Togodumnus. He left a garrison there and moved forward.' It is generally accepted by scholars that the Bodunni are in fact a mis-spelling or scribal error for the Dobunni of Gloucestershire and surrounding areas. Although written some 150 years after the conquest, the reference may indicate that at least part of the area adopted a pro-Roman stance. The archaeological evidence from the Cirencester area is especially important here; the late Iron Age *oppidum* at Bagendon continued to thrive for at least 20 years after the Roman conquest and the earliest romanised 'villa' like stone building in the region was built over the adjacent late Iron Age settlement at The Ditches. This dates to around 60-70AD and may be the residence of a pro-Roman local leader who made an early decision to adopt a Roman lifestyle.

An earth and timber Roman fort was constructed 8km to the south of Bagendon at Cirencester, the first significant occupation of the site, from about AD44 or 45. Two early Roman tombstones from Cirencester attest to at least two Auxiliary cavalry regiments being present during the 25 years the fort was in use. One names Genialis, (Figure 16) a trooper born close to the modern Dutch-Belgian border, serving in a Thracian cavalry regiment originally raised in the Balkans. The second is of a cavalryman named Dannicus serving in the Ala Indiana Gallorum, a unit originally from eastern France close to the German border. The Cirencester fort was sited on what became a major road junction of the Fosse Way linking fortresses at Exeter and Lincoln with another route cutting across the Cotswold Hills towards the River Severn at Gloucester. A legionary fortress was established at Kingsholm by AD48 or 49 and subsequently moved a short distance to the site of modern Gloucester in the mid 60s. These successive bases were used as the springboard for the Roman advance into south Wales.

As with most early Roman forts, the presence of a garrison soon attracted both local and provincial civilians who occupied a settlement beyond the fort perimeter. Known as a *vicus*, these settlements often grew and developed into towns on the departure of the army. This was certainly the case at Cirencester where following the departure of the army, probably in the early 70s AD, the site was developed as a romanised city acting as a tribal centre or *civitas*, similar in function to a modern county town.

Closer to Box an early Roman fort must have existed at Bath to guard the strategically important crossing of the Fosse Way over the River Avon. The precise location remains uncertain although much early Roman material has been recorded from the Walcot Street area and a fort has been postulated at Bathwick, close to where the modern Cleveland Bridge crosses the River Avon.

Other early Roman military sites in the region are known at Ilchester in Somerset, at Sea Mills near Avonmouth (a ferry point for crossing to south Wales) and others are suspected near Marlborough and Westbury in Wiltshire. Based on the current evidence, the pattern overall for the region would suggest little resistance to the invading forces as the known early Roman garrisons are widely spaced.

The establishment of the Roman road network

ONCE THE REGION was considered secure, work could commence on organizing the new province. An early feature of the romanised landscape will have been the construction of the main road network. Built initially to facilitate rapid movement of troops and officials, these well-built highways will have rapidly become important for regional economic development. As yet we do not have any close dating for their construction but we may assume that once the region was considered to be secure the

19 The Fosse Way to the north-east of Colerne

military surveyors and engineers will have commenced work. For our region this probably had begun by 50 to 55AD. There are two main routes which pass close to Box en route to Bath. The Fosse Way, running from south-west to north-east linking Exeter with Lincoln (Figure 19) and an east-west route running from London, the provincial capital after the rebellion of Boudicca in AD60-61, to Sea Mills near Avonmouth. A third, probably less important route, is known to have branched from the Fosse Way south of Bath and run in a south-easterly direction towards Poole Harbour.

The Fosse way passes some three kilometres to the west of Box and the London-Sea Mills route two kilometres to the south. The major routes are carefully surveyed and engineered with a cambered, gravel metalled surface. Many of the roads can still be traced today often surviving as modern routes, green lanes, footpaths or parish boundaries. The minor roads which will have provided local access are less well constructed and consequently harder to identify. Across much of Roman Britain we still lack the detailed map of the communications network away from the main roads.

Roman Bath

ROMAN OCCUPATION IN Bath almost certainly began as a temporary earth and timber fort on the line of the Fosse Way. A pre-Roman settlement had existed here; traces of round houses have been excavated at Lower Common Allotments and there are Iron Age coins from the springs beside the Roman Baths. The Roman name of the site, *Aquae Sulis* – the 'Waters of Sulis' includes the name of the local goddess Sulis and this name is of British origin.

The therapeutic nature of the water issuing from the geo-thermal springs were soon noted by the earliest Roman population of Bath. Within a few decades of the conquest, possibly as early as the mid 60s AD, a major building programme commenced with the construction of a temple within a sacred precinct or Temenos, a large suite of baths and numerous other buildings. These were developed, enlarged and maintained throughout the Roman period and the temple, dedicated to the goddess Sulis-Minerva, was one of only a few temples of true classical design in Roman Britain. Much of the decorated stone triangular pediment of the temple has been recovered and a gilt bronze head found in the eighteenth century depicts the goddess Sulis-Minerva. The early construction date for the complex coupled with a dedication including the Roman goddess Minerva (guardian deity of the Roman state) strongly suggests that the Roman Army played a key role in the development of the complex. The style of many of the architectural features also suggests the presence of skilled stonemasons from southern France or northern Italy. In all probability the development of the religious spa at *Aquae Sulis* was initially under military sponsorship, and some archaeologists have even suggested that during the Roman conquest of Wales Bath was in effect a 'rest and recuperation' centre for troops. A continuing army interest in Bath is evidenced by the large number of tombstones and altars found in the city to serving and retired military personnel. As the site developed it attracted both pilgrims and officiating priests from many parts of the Empire. In the early third century the site was mentioned by the writer Solinus who recorded the burning of 'stones' upon the altars to the goddess; almost certainly a reference to the use of coal from the nearby North Somerset coal measures.

The main area of the bathing and temple complex covered an area of approximately ten hectares (25 acres) and towards the end of the Roman period this core was enclosed by a stone wall (Figure 20).

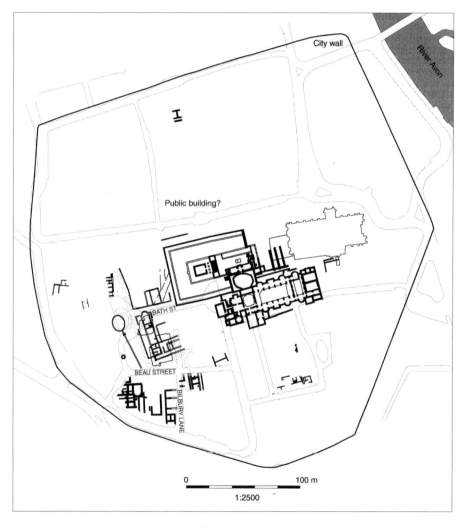

20 Plan of Roman Bath

The defences did not incorporate all of the built up area and an extensive settlement is also known along the line of modern Walcot Street. It is now thought that the stone defences enclosed a primarily religious area and the main secular settlement was that along Walcot Street.

The Roman complex at Bath was the nearest urban centre to the villa at Box. Although clearly a highly specialized religious healing centre, it will also have served as a local administrative and market centre. The attractions of the baths and temples at the site will have acted as an important stimulus to the local economy drawing on the resources of the surrounding landscape and providing access to many luxury goods, services and ideas from across the Roman Empire. The wealth of inscriptions from Bath, on tombstones, altars and other monuments provide graphic evidence of the cosmopolitan nature of the residents and visitors to the town, all of whom must have had an influence on the local population.

Military personnel rank high on the list of those commemorated. These include Marcus Valerius Latinus of the Twentieth Legion, born in Nyon in modern Switzerland; Gaius Murrius of the Second Adiutrix Legion from modern Frejus in southern France, Lucius Vitellius Tancinus, a cavalryman from central Spain and Julius Vitalis, an armourer of the Twentieth Legion from northern France. Other individuals commemorated include Peregrinus from the Moselle region of western Germany; Priscus, a stonemason from the area of modern Chartres; a lady named Rusonia Aventina from the Metz region of eastern France and Antigonus from Nicopolis, close to the modern Greek-Albanian border. Locals are also recorded; these include two different individuals named Sulinus, presumably after the goddess Sulis. One, named as 'Sulinus the son of Brucetus', described himself as a sculptor and is also recorded on an altar from Cirencester. More personal and poignant memorials are also known. There is one to Mercatilla who lived 1 year, 5 months and 12 days and Successa Petronia who lived 3 years, 4 months and 9 days. The tombstone of a priest of the Goddess Sulis is recorded from Bathwick. He is named as Gaius Calpurnius Receptus who died aged 75. The memorial was erected by his wife, Calpurnia Trifosa, freedwomen (ex-slave). Two further inscriptions are worth recording. A statue base found in 1965 bears the inscription 'To the Goddess Sulis, Marcus Lucius Memor, augurer, gave this gift'. An augurer divined the future by examining the organs of sacrificed animals and came from a tradition with origins in Etruscan religion. An altar, found in Stall Street in 1753, carries an inscription recording an act of desecration; it reads 'This holy spot, wrecked by insolent hands and cleansed afresh, Gaius Severius

Emeritus, centurion in charge of the region, has restored to the Virtue and Deity of the Emperor'.

In addition to the formal memorials, the Sacred Spring at Bath has produced over one hundred pieces of lead on to which curses have been written and then thrown to the goddess for action. These give a wonderful personal insight into the lives and beliefs of many individuals. A flavour of the curses is given by these few examples: 'Docilianus . . . to the most holy goddess Sulis. I curse him who has stolen my hooded cloak, whether man or woman, whether slave or free, that . . . the goddess Sulis inflict death upon . . . and not allow him sleep or children now and in the future, until he has brought my hooded cloak to the temple of her divinity.' 'To the goddess Sulis Minerva. I ask your most sacred majesty that you take vengeance on those who have done [me] wrong, that you permit them neither sleep . . .' Others record the theft of a glove and another, probably of fourth century date, refers to both pagans and Christians.

In addition to religious and healing services Bath has produced evidence for industrial activities including lead and iron working as well as exploitation of the local fine-grained limestone for building and sculpture. The lead (and the lead alloy, pewter) known to have been produced in Roman Bath will no doubt have been supplied from the lead mines on Mendip, notably the large deposits around Charterhouse. A Roman period village on Lansdown, north of Bath and close to the present race course, has produced stone moulds for the casting of pewter vessels. Iron occurs relatively locally in North Somerset and coal from the same area may have fuelled the furnaces.

A major centre such as Bath also acted as a major market focus for villas and other substantial country buildings. At least thirty examples are known so far within a 25 kilometre (16 miles) radius of the town, the Box villa being the largest recorded to date.

3
The Origins of the Villa

What is a villa?

THE TERM 'VILLA' is used in Roman Britain to describe a broad range of country dwellings; there are approximately 1,100 known buildings termed as 'villas'. These can range from very simple buildings comprising no more than three or four rooms, maybe with a linking corridor; large complexes built around a courtyard such as Chedworth or Box, to palatial structures like Woodchester near Stroud, comparable in size to the Duke of Marlborough's seat at Blenheim Palace. The villas of Roman Britain are largely restricted to the lowland zone away from the areas which remained under military control and reflecting the more fertile soils (Figure 21). Within the lowland zone the distribution of villas is far from even and there are significant clusters around towns such as Bath, Cirencester, Ilchester and St Albans.

The villas of Britain are different from those found at the heart of the Empire where the tradition of owning a rural estate or luxurious retreat dates back to the period of the Roman Republic in the third and second centuries BC. We have no contemporary Roman texts describing villas in Britain and although the British examples are romanised in construction and décor we can recognise a series of regional types and styles.

The majority of the villas in Roman Britain were associated with farming. Where excavation has been undertaken and revealed the full plan of the villa we can identify barns, granaries, smithies and other activities we would expect to see on an agricultural estate centre.

Who lived in the villas?

ROMAN PROVINCIAL ADMINISTRATION was largely by delegation. A provincial Governor and his staff would be appointed by the Emperor,

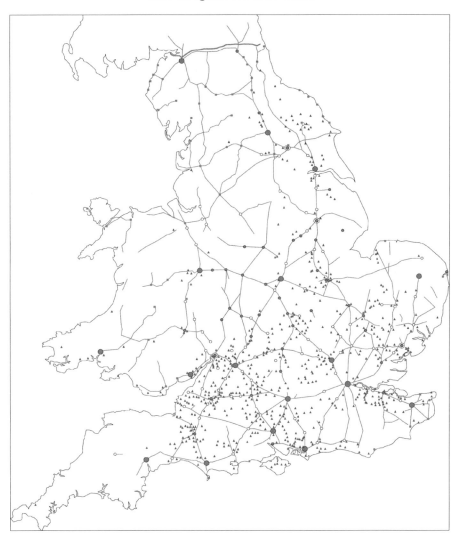

21 The distribution of villas in Roman Britain also showing the main roads and towns

usually from the Roman aristocracy. Below the Governor, where practicable, Rome would use the local ruling families, often granting them citizenship and installing them in positions of responsibility. In Britain many of these families would be the descendants of Iron Age tribal leaders; they probably sat on city and tribal councils and were encouraged to adopt Roman customs. Although these indigenous families will have owned substantial townhouses their main home would be the villa and the dependent estate their main source of income. This part of Romano-British society formed the majority of private landholders. Other villas will have been owned by retired soldiers, immigrants from other parts of the Empire, officials and some estates will have belonged to the Emperor.

We know the names of only a few villa owners in Britain. One, the 'Villa Faustini', is named on the early third century AD road map, the Antonine Itinerary, and is thought to be located near Scole in Norfolk. Another is the Lady Melania (later canonised as St Melania the Younger) an aristocratic woman born around 383AD. In her biography it is recorded that Melania disposed of all her estates around the empire, including those in Britain, to lead the life of a Christian ascetic. It is quite probable that she had never visited her British estates and we do not know where they were located. From a villa at Thruxton in Hampshire a fourth century AD mosaic bears an inscription giving the name 'QVINTVS NATALIVS NATALINVS ET BODENI', this is thought to be the name of the owner (Figure 22).

The personal financial liability of holding public office became increasingly severe in the later Roman period, with many of the aristocrats and the landed classes withdrawing to their villa estates to escape the burden. The majority of the developed and well-appointed villas in Roman Britain date from the mid third and fourth centuries AD and may partly reflect this urban exodus, although many

22 *Mosaic from Thruxton in Hampshire with inscription giving a name thought to be of the villa owner.*

of the sites may have earlier origins. For example, in Hampshire and central Wessex many villas have been demonstrated to lie directly on top of major late Iron Age farms, and excavation has demonstrated continuity from the Iron Age into the Roman period.

A further aspect of 'villa' settlement should be introduced; their additional function as a religious centre. If a villa acted as an estate centre then it may be compared to an eighteenth-century English large country house where a church or chapel was provided for the religious needs of the family, estate workers and other dependants. A number of villas have produced evidence for a religious focus. At Bancroft near Milton Keynes and

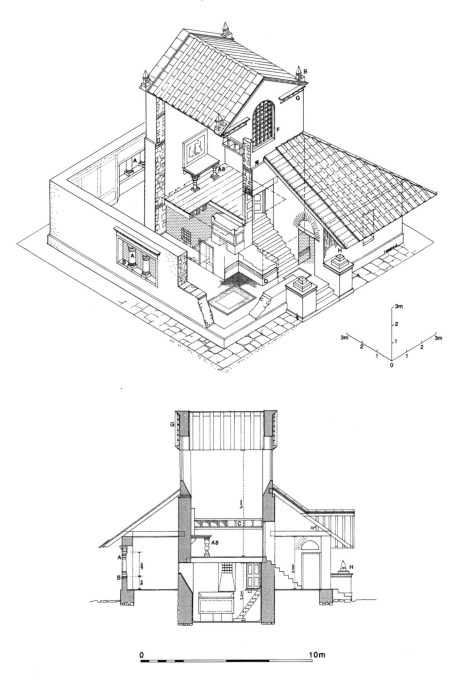

23 Reconstruction of a temple/mausoleum of Romano-Celtic type at the Bancroft Roman villa in Buckinghamshire (after Williams and Zeepvat 1994)

Lullingstone in Kent there are mausolea, probably family tombs which were also used as a place of worship. In Britain these take the form of a Romano-Celtic temple. This type of building, usually comprising a tall inner square structure surrounded by an ambulatory or corridor, is mainly confined to Britain and northern France (Figure 23).

During the fourth century AD phase of the Lullingstone villa a Christian chapel was created in the house, presumably for private family worship.

Other villas have been suggested as serving as large rural religious centres and retreats rather than mere country houses. This function has been proposed for the large villa at Chedworth near Cirencester with the house re-interpreted as a well-appointed guest house for wealthy pilgrims. At least two large probable temples are known near to the main building complex and the presence of a 'Nymphaeum' or water shrine around an adjacent spring is taken as further evidence of a religious function. At Gadebridge Park near Hemel Hempstead in Hertfordshire, a large open air swimming pool fed by mineral springs close to the villa is thought to be part of a healing shrine. Not all accept this interpretation, although any large country house in the Roman period is likely to have functioned at a number of levels.

The springs, silver eye and various pieces of sculpture from Box have led some to suggest that this villa too may have had a religious focus; this is discussed and developed further in Chapter Five.

Early Roman villas in Britain

THE MAJORITY OF early Roman stone-built villas in Britain are to be found in the south-east of the country and are relatively rare. They include sites such as Eccles in Kent, Angmering, Pulborough and Fishbourne in Sussex. The latter site is palatial in character and exceptional by British standards. During the second century AD a number of stone villas were built in the St Albans area and the Darenth Valley in Kent. Well known examples include Gadebridge Park near Hemel Hempstead in Hertfordshire and Lullingstone in Kent.

In western Britain the majority of the known villa plans reflect their maximum extent, probably reached during the fourth century AD. Many of these sites were first investigated in the nineteenth century with little or no archaeological recording and the full sequence is difficult to unravel without further excavation. Analysis of the plans can provide a hint of building phases but precise dating is difficult without reference to more recently excavated sites. At a number of villas excavated in the last few decades it is possible to see a long and often complex sequence of development. At Frocester Court, between Gloucester and Stroud, excavation has revealed a complex development beginning in the Late Bronze Age, circa 1,000-700BC and continuing into the Iron Age with a succession of ditched enclosures with timber roundhouses. The site continues after the Roman conquest with rectangular timber buildings dating from circa 100AD to 275AD. It is only at around 275AD that the first stone villa buildings with mosaics and painted wall plaster are erected. Where occupation from the Iron Age into the Roman period can be demonstrated it is tempting to interpret this as evidence for continuity of ownership within the increasingly romanised indigenous population, which was gradually accruing wealth to allow building in Roman fashion. However, without absolute evidence for continuity of tenure this can, at best, only remain an assumption.

The Late Iron Age
and Early Roman Period at Box

THE RELIABILITY AND volume of the water supply provided by the springs feeding the tufa terrace at Box make it an attractive focus for settlement. Use of the location in the Mesolithic and Neolithic periods is attested by worked flint tools, and Bronze Age burial mounds (round barrows) overlooking Box on Kingsdown show that people were living and dying in the area at that time.

The only evidence for Late Iron Age activity from Box is a single gold Iron Age coin found in the grounds of Box House and a glass bangle from The Hermitage. Pottery and a saddle quern (corn grinder) of Iron Age type are recorded from Ditteridge. Evidence for Iron Age occupation is otherwise lacking but the existence of a settlement of this date may still await discovery. Further away from Box there are cropmarks of Iron Age type settlements to the north and south of the village as well as the hillforts described in Chapter Two.

The remains of the villa excavated in the nineteenth century are those of the later Roman house, probably built around 270 to 300AD. Subsequent analysis of the phasing based largely on Harold Brakspear's plan and the 1967-8 excavations led to the suggestion that the core of the villa was first built during the middle of the 2nd century AD. A recent re-examination of the pottery suggests this date may now be slightly later and belong to the opening decades of the third century AD (see below).

The earliest Roman material from the site comes from approximately

100 metres to the south-west of the later villa; recovered from an earlier Roman ditch excavated in the grounds of The Hermitage in 1982 by Mrs Kate Carless. This material includes 18 kilos of ceramic building debris, a tufa voussoir (component from an arch or vault), vessel and window glass, and 49.2 kilos of pottery. Amongst the material was a small silver object in the form of a human eye. The potential significance of this object is discussed further in Chapter Five.

This discovery in The Hermitage is very important. The pottery assemblage is the earliest group from Box and contains material which may have accumulated over 150 years with much material dated to the later first and second century AD. Due to advances in pottery dating since the ditch was excavated and the investigations of 1967-8 the overall dating of this material can be reassessed. The very latest pottery is of the early third century AD suggesting a date of about 200-220AD for its final deposition. The ditch deposit may be associated with the general levelling and tidying up of the area prior to the construction of the first phase of the known villa. Some further pottery and building debris, possibly contemporary with The Hermitage ditch material, was recovered from below the north-east corner of the later villa in 1967. These deposits leave little doubt that an earlier and potentially quite substantial Roman building had stood somewhere in the vicinity although the precise location of this remains unknown.

The reassessment of these two key groups of artefacts suggests that the first phase of the stone building successively excavated between 1829 and 1967 must date from the very late second or, more likely the earlier third century AD rather than the mid-second century as originally proposed.

The First Stone Villa

THE ORIGINAL BOX villa plan, following the proposal put forward by Hurst, is of a south facing building flanked by wings surrounded by a corridor or *porticus*. This will have comprised rooms 1, 21, 29, 41 (corridors), 3-10 (the North Range), 12, 14, 15 (the East Range) and 36-38 (the West Range; Figure 24). Whether this first phase villa had a series of associated outbuildings is uncertain but it may be suspected that these will have been present. The bath-suite in the East Range (rooms 30-35), based upon the plan and the style of their associated mosaics, is probably later in date and belongs to the aggrandised fourth century villa (see below). An earlier bath-suite, quite possibly detached from the main house, must still await discovery. The topography of the site argues against such a bath-suite being

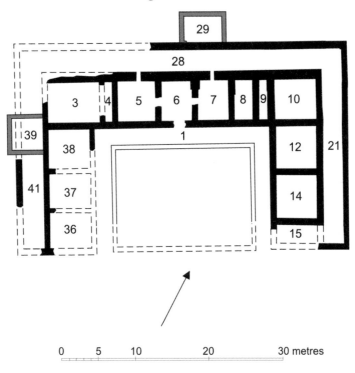

24 *Reconstructed plan of the Phase 1 Box villa*

located to the north of the villa. It is possible that it lay to the south of the East Range, possibly under the churchyard where antiquarian records suggest the presence of further Roman structures. This location is also in close proximity to springs which rise to the east and south of the church and would have provided the necessary water supply.

The recovery of loose tesserae in the 1967-8 excavations make it clear that the first stone phase house did have mosaics although none survived intact (the known and surviving examples can be dated to the later Roman period on stylistic grounds). The house also had glazed windows, based on the discovery of

25 *Reconstruction of part of a Roman ceramic roof constructed from flat and curving tiles displayed at the Roman Legionary Museum at Caerleon near Newport in South Wales. On the tile to the right you can make out the imprint of the hob-nailed sole of a shoe where someone has walked across it before it was fired.*

fragments of window glass; it had painted plaster on the interior walls and the roof was possibly of ceramic tiles (Figure 25). It is not impossible that this villa replaced an even earlier building, built largely of timber, of which no archaeological trace has yet been recognised apart from the debris recovered from The Hermitage ditch and below the later villa. Although we cannot be absolutely certain, it is likely that the original house was also provided with heated rooms. In all probability these were same rooms, number 5 and 7, which had hypocausts and mosaics in the late Roman house.

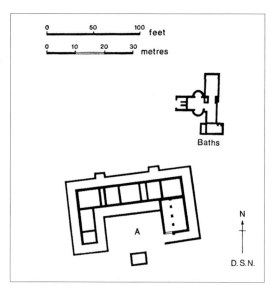

26 *Gadebridge Park villa, Hertfordshire, Period 3 (after Neal 1974)*

The plan of the Phase 1 Box villa has strong similarities with the plan of a late second century AD villa at Gadebridge Park, Hemel Hempstead in Hertfordshire (Figure 26). During this phase the Gadebridge Park villa had a detached bath-suite. This is a relatively common feature of earlier villas and is probably to minimise the fire risk, as many early villas may have had a timber framed upper structure resting on low stone walls. A further similar ground plan of broadly similar date is also known from the villa at Ditchley in Oxfordshire.

The date of the addition of projecting rooms 29 and 39 to the North and West Ranges at Box is uncertain, but they may be additions of the third century prior to the major works of the early fourth century and the construction of room 26. Room 39 is the only heated room in the West Range and its addition will have provided it with a level of comfort hitherto restricted to the North Range. The floor of room 39 had been supported on brick-built pillars, called *pilae*, and the recovery of many loose tesserae shows that it, like the heated rooms 7 and 9, had also once been furnished with a fine mosaic floor. Room 29 was in a poor state of preservation and we do not know whether it originally had a mosaic floor.

The change in facilities marked by the addition of rooms 29 and 39 may also reflect a change in the social structure of the villa. Writing in 1978 the architectural historian J.T. Smith identified 'unit' type villa houses where suites of rooms, or units, usually arranged in blocks of three, were identified as self-contained dwellings within the larger villa plan. In developing this theme it has also been noted that one unit, or suite of units, is frequently larger or better appointed. This is interpreted as a reflection of joint proprietorship, possibly based on the extended family model with 'senior' and 'cadet' branches of the same family sharing the villa house, the estate and common resources. This model or theory sees the 'senior' branch as having access to the higher quality accommodation block. At some sites, where we have the full villa plan, two bath-suites are also known, one larger and better appointed than the second. The pattern of larger and smaller 'units' is widely recognisable in building plans across the villa zones of Britain, northern France and parts of the Rhineland. Smith has further suggested that this distinctive feature may be a reflection of pre-Roman conquest social practices. Although not universally accepted, this interpretation has much to commend it in explaining the development of villa buildings as a shared resource. If this pattern is accepted for Box, the addition of rooms 29 and 39 may reflect the growing complexity of tenure and the need to accommodate a growing extended family with aspirations within provincial society. The North Range will have remained the dominant part of the house with two heated rooms (5 and 7) and room 6 as the main reception room. The addition of Room 29 could be interpreted as a private summer *triclinium* or dining room taking advantage of the extensive and dramatic views to the north across the valley of the By Brook. Although undated, the logical sequence would be to place these modifications earlier than the rebuilding of the north-east corner with the addition of the large apsidal chamber, room 26. We may then tentatively assign these rooms to some point in the middle to later third century AD before the major remodelling.

Whatever the function of the different wings in the first stone villa, it is clear that further structures must await discovery at Box. As we have already seen, villas are primarily estate centres, engaged in farming and using the surplus produce from that farming to maintain the family life style. Fully excavated sites feature barns, work halls and other agrarian buildings – all a prerequisite of a large working farm or estate centre. Examples of this may be seen in the plan of the nearby villa at Atworth (below, p 83). Such out-buildings have yet to be located or identified at Box.

By the end of the third century AD further changes are evident at Box. These mark the elevation of the house from a comfortable rural residence into a distinctive type of site that is frequently referred to as 'a seat of lordship' with a large and imposing 'audience chamber' with a curved apse at one end, here represented by room 26, the laying of highly decorative and expensive mosaic floors and all the trappings of the late Roman wealthy landed class. In this phase Box develops into a major centre and, in addition to being a wealthy residence, may also have developed a further function as a religious site and a place of pilgrimage. Most of the site excavated in 1902 and 1903 and published by Sir Harold Brakspear belongs to this late Roman phase. The description of the remains, the possible function, status and appearance of this grand house are discussed in the next chapter.

4

The Later Roman Villa Complex

IF WE COULD transport ourselves backwards in time to the year 350AD, stand on the slopes above the north bank of the By Brook and look to the south, we would have seen an astonishing sight. Occupying the ground where The Wilderness, Box House and Box church now stand would have been a very large, probably multi-storied, range of buildings terraced into the hillside. A two-storied façade, over 44 metres (140 feet) in length would have run from left to right with a massive buttressed hall standing high over the left (eastern) end. The upper part of the façade may have been an open terrace with a roof supported on dwarf limestone pillars with views over a terraced garden. This was the rear, probably the private range, of the massive Roman building whose construction commenced towards the end of the third century AD and turned the earlier villa into a complex of near palatial proportions. At its greatest extent, the Box villa would have had at least fifty rooms at ground level, probably with further chambers on an upper storey (Figure 27). The original short projecting wings on the east and west were extended to the south, probably around one or more courtyards. Whether there was a fourth range closing the south side remains unknown as the present church and graveyard occupy this area. Of the fifty or so rooms known, at least twenty had mosaic floors, all with geometric patterns, and a large bath-suite was constructed in the east range. Additional buildings are known in the grounds of Box House and below the Vicarage, to the west and east of the villa core. These were also part of the aggrandised fourth century complex but may have had different functions.

Each of the ranges will be briefly described here and their salient features and function discussed.

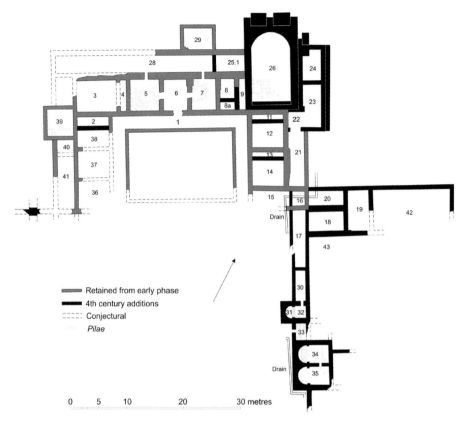

27 Box Villa: plan of the fourth century villa when at its greatest extent

The Fourth Century House

The North Range

ALL OF THE north range was retained from the earlier building but it was extended in length by the addition of rooms 23, 24 and 26. Now 44 metres (140 feet) long and 14 metres (46 feet) wide it faced south into a courtyard and the fronting corridor, room 1, continued around the inner sides of the west and east ranges. Room 1 would have given access to most of the rooms on the ground floor of the villa. As part of the remodelling of the house the corridor was provided with a mosaic floor comprising

28 Part of the Pelta mosaic design in Room 1 as recorded by Sir Harold Brakspear

a continuous pelta design framed by dark grey/blue bands within a white border (Figure 28). The presence of a mosaic floor in this corridor suggests that this space was fully enclosed and probably lit by glazed windows. Some reconstructions of Roman villas show these corridors as being open to the elements, comprising low stone walls with dwarf columns supporting a lean-to roof. The presence of a mosaic floor makes this unlikely in the case of Box as the winter effects of damp and frost would rapidly affect the mortar base of the floor and cause serious damage. The complexity of the geometric design is also unusual for a corridor and may be seen as a statement by the villa owners of their wealth and taste.

29 Mosaic floor in Room 6 as recorded by Sir Harold Brakspear

Of the nine rooms that formed the core of the north range, at least seven were provided with mosaic floors and two had hypocausted under-floor heating systems. The central room, 6, was provided with a very fine mosaic floor. This is one of the floors first exposed by Hardy in 1898 and left open to the elements, subsequently suffering from frost damage. The surviving portion of the floor was recorded in detail by Sir Harold Brakspear and the design shows it was of a complex geometric form with circular panels within octagons, squares and lozenges (Figure 29). The central position of

30 Room 5 as excavated looking south showing the stone hypocaust supports for the floor

this room within the range allows identification as a formal reception room also used as the summer dining area or *triclinium*. Here the owner would receive and entertain important guests. To either side of room 6 are a pair of heated rooms, 5 and 7. Both of these rooms originally had mosaic floors but had been destroyed. The floors were supported by stone blocks known as *pilae* which allowed the warm air to circulate beneath them (Figure 30). Hollow bricks built into the walls allowed the warm air to rise providing a comfortable all round heat. These heated rooms will have acted as winter reception and dining areas.

Fragments of mosaic floors survived in rooms 3 and 4 at the west end. The floor in room 4, a narrow passage probably providing access to the rooms on either side, was a simple geometric design of a swastika meander (Figure 31). In room 3 only fragments of the border survived.

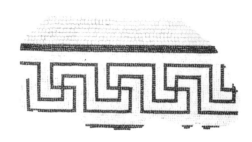

31 Mosaic floor in room 4.

At the eastern end of the range, in room 8, a near complete mosaic survived featuring a central knot design surrounded by a swastika meander (Figure

32). This was lifted in 1898 and is now lost, although Hardy made a tracing of it before it was removed. The room also appears to have had painted walls and large amounts of yellow painted wall-plaster were noted. Room 9, a narrow corridor of similar dimensions to room 4, also had a simple geometric design mosaic floor with a chequer design in dark brown surrounded by a buff border.

32 Mosaic floor in Room 8

The West Range

IN THE WEST range there is little evidence for major changes. The general survival of the range was poor and it had been damaged by the construction of a later Medieval mill and leat system. Room 2, a narrow passage linking room 1 with heated room 39, was provided with a simple geometric mosaic. The fragmentary remains of this were formerly covered by a trapdoor in the lawn of The Wilderness garden but this has now been removed. No floor levels survived in the other rooms although loose tesserae in room 39 show that this once had a mosaic. The west range must have extended further to the south than is currently known and the antiquarian references to discoveries, including mosaics, in the churchyard support this.

The Grand Chamber – Room 26

THE MOST SUBSTANTIAL addition to the fourth century house was the construction of a massive chamber on to the corner of the complex where the north and east ranges meet. The groundworks for this included the creation of a massive earth and rubble platform over 2m in thick. The room, numbered 26, had walls 1.2 metres (4 feet) thick and an apse with an internal diameter of 6.8 metres (just over 22 feet) at the north end. The room measured 7 metres (23 feet) from east to west, 12.5 metres (just over 40 feet) from north to south and had a hypocaust with a mosaic floor. Little

33 The buttressed foundation of room 26 as excavated. View to the southeast

of the mosaic survived although Brakspear's description of 'fine tesserae' suggests that it was of high quality. The north wall of this grand chamber projected downslope from the main range and was supported by three large buttresses built in fine limestone blocks (Figure 33).

The thrust from the weight of this room was evidently miscalculated by the builders and required additional buttressing to the north wall, and the width of east wall was increased to 1.95 metres (just over 6 feet). The scale of the surviving foundations for this room leave little doubt that it was a major addition to the house and will have had a very special purpose. The diameter of the apse at Box is the second largest known in a Romano-British domestic structure, only bettered by an example from Aldborough in Yorkshire, the Roman town of *Isurium*.

In appearance this chamber will have been a very tall structure and probably had an internal vaulted ceiling with a hipped, tiled roof over it. The height, from the floor to the top of the vaulted ceiling, although conjectural, must have been at least 14 metres (46 feet) based upon standard Roman architectural rules of proportion.

The room may have been provided with two entrances; one being a private access from the north range by way of room 28, and the other a public entrance on the east side where a pair of rooms, 23 and 24, could act as an entrance lobby and waiting space. In one of these, room 23, part of a quality sculpture depicting a hunter god was found (Figure 34). Whether the complete sculpture was once displayed in this room or, as Sir Harold Brakspear suggested, the surviving block had merely been used in the make-up for the floor, remains uncertain.

34 *Relief of a hunter god found in Room 23. The surviving part shows a male figure with a deer across the shoulders*

Rooms on this scale occur only in the grandest of later Roman houses across the Empire and were clearly inspired by the great audience chambers that featured in late Roman Imperial palaces such as Trier in Germany and Split on the Adriatic coast (Figure 35).

Large rooms of this type are known at a number of villa sites in Roman Britain. These invariably are the larger and most richly appointed villas in a region and they provide a clue to the status and aspirations of the villa owners. By the late Roman period wealthy provincial landowners had become increasingly powerful and would be expected publicly to receive actual and potential political allies. In addition this class had also acquired significant powers over their tenants and workforce, with the peasant class effectively tied to the estate. From this chamber the owner would also adjudicate in local disputes between members of his extended family, tenants and other dependants. These functions have been argued as an identifier for a villa being a seat of power or lordship similar to that of a great Medieval lord. Comparisons can also be made with the exercise of power and public hospitality in English

35 *An early fourth century Imperial audience chamber, the Aula Palatina, at Trier in Germany. This remarkable survival of a late Roman building gives an impression of how room 26 may have appeared*

country houses of the eighteenth and nineteenth centuries where large public reception rooms are a prominent architectural feature. The construction and scale of room 26 is powerful evidence for the transformation of the Box villa into a major estate centre during the first half of the fourth century.

An alternative interpretation would be to view the chamber as a meeting and dining room used for religious ceremonies associated with the so called 'mystery cults', including the cult of the god Bacchus. Despite the growing popularity of Christianity, eastern Mediterranean cults were popular during the first half of the fourth century amongst the wealthy and educated class. Devotees would meet in private chambers, decorated with figured mosaics, often depicting the Orpheus myth, to feast and worship.

While we cannot be absolutely certain about the use of room 26 (and indeed it may have served a number of functions), use as a public chamber for formal meetings and the exercise of authority is the most attractive.

The decoration of rooms like number 26 were designed to reflect not only the power and status of the owner but also his level of romanisation and education in Roman mythology and its associated symbolism. This is a feature recently underscored by the discovery of a large villa with an imposing reception room at the junction of two ranges at Dinnington, near Ilminster in Somerset. Like Box, this was a heated room and the fragments of mosaic recovered have been identified as a depiction of Daphne transformed into a laurel bush. This is the climax of a story by the Roman writer Ovid from his *Metamorphoses* and is a graphic demonstration of the classical knowledge and interests of the villa owner. Whilst we have no evidence for the design of the mosaic in Room 26, it is likely to have been a high quality floor with designs and themes designed to reflect the intellectual interests (real or aspired) of the owner.

One of the very few datable finds recorded from the Hardy excavation came from the fill of the hypocaust in Room 26 were the fragmentary remains of a pewter jug, now lost. The description given in the 1904 report allows it to be identified as a well-known type considered as 4th century AD in date. Vessels of similar form have been recovered from Bath and may well have been made locally using Mendip lead (Figure 36).

36 Pair of pewter jugs found at Bath

The East Range and the Baths

THE EAST RANGE was at least 50 metres (164 feet) long and towards the southern end was a large and well constructed bath-suite excavated in 1881. Like the west range, the northern part of the east range was a central block of rooms flanked by an inner and outer corridor, room 1 and room 21. Five rooms are known, two of which, 11 and 13, were narrow corridors and could be interpreted as stair wells for access to an upper storey. In the southernmost room, 15, traces of a mosaic floor survived and a miniature stone altar was found but no trace of an inscription survived.

The pond in the grounds of The Wilderness and an existing boundary wall made investigation of the main range beyond room 15 impossible, but a southern continuation of the outer corridor is known and this provided access to the bath-suite. The bath-suite was large but the full plan has yet to be established, and it must continue into the front garden of The Vicarage. The baths were accessed by a long narrow corridor, rooms 18 and 30. In room 30 a well-preserved mosaic featuring a geometric design was uncovered and then removed for display by Mr Stier (Figures 37 and 38).

37 View of Room 31 (foreground) and Room 30 as uncovered in 1881. The apsidal feature to the left is the cold-plunge bath

The mosaic continued into rooms 31 and 32 and these were the cold rooms, or frigidarium, of the bath-suite, complete with a small plunge bath set in an apse. The account of the discovery of the baths specifically records that the plunge bath still had traces of mosaic on its sides; a rare survival in Roman Britain. Beyond room 31 were at least three heated rooms, 33, 34 and 35.

To enter room 33 required the bather to ascend two steps as the ground level gently rises to the south (Figure 39).

The floors were missing but many of the supporting brick piers survived. It is probable that these rooms were originally furnished with mosaics and a number of fragments were recovered depicting rows in dark purple-red, red and white. The normal sequence of Roman bathing ran from cold, through warm to hot rooms and it is most likely that room 33 was the warm room or

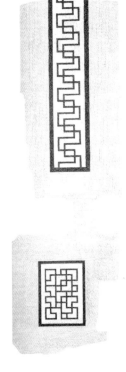

tepidarium and rooms 34 and 35, each with an apse on the west side, the hot rooms or caldarium. It is most likely that the apses once housed hot plunge baths. The furnace areas have not been located, but may be to the east or south of the known rooms and will have supported a large bronze boiler providing hot water to the baths. The water supply for the baths would have been provided by the spring which still rises close by the east gate into the churchyard.

Substantial stone drains run around the west side of the suite and demonstrate the care and attention given by the builders to the water supply and drainage systems. The plan of the bath-suite is clearly incomplete and traces of walling running east and south from rooms 34 and 35 show that there are further rooms awaiting discovery.

Bathing in the Roman world was an important part of social life as well as for the maintenance of personal hygiene. The scale of the east baths at Box show that they were an important part of the complex.

38 Mosaic floor in Rooms 30 and 31 (from Cosh and Neal 2005)

The overall size of the Box villa would strongly suggest that there was more than one bath-suite, in keeping with other large villas known in western Britain. There are at least two suites at Chedworth near Cirencester, and at North Leigh in Oxfordshire three are known. We may speculate that another bath-suite will have been present at Box and a possible location would be under the present churchyard, close to the springs which fed the known baths.

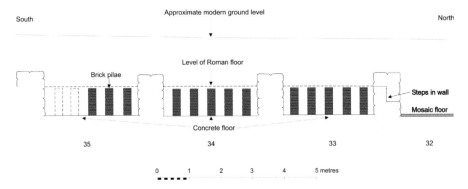

39 Section through the bath suite showing the change in floor levels

Although we have few surviving records of the interior décor of the villa, many fragments of painted wall plaster were noted during the earlier excavations. The colours, in keeping with Roman taste, are bold and include shades of red, yellow, green, black and white. The identifiable schemes include foliage and panels imitating marble veneers. In some instances evidence of redecoration is provided by multiple layers of painted plaster. Some of the fragments are derived from the earlier house on the site and only survived when they were accidently incorporated in material dumped to make up levels for the late Roman building. A late nineteenth century watercolour shows

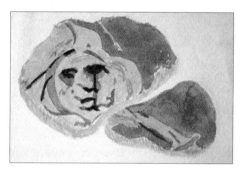

one fragment with part of a human figure and recorded as being 'in the possession of Mr Falconer' (Figure 40). Unfortunately this piece is now lost and the watercolour is the only record. It is quite likely that some of the painted plaster fragments are also derived from decorated ceilings.

40 Nineteenth century watercolour of painted wall plaster from Box depicting part of a human figure

The exterior of the villa was also plastered and traces of this, in a cream colour, survived on the outer face of the North Range close to room 26. The late Roman enlargement of the villa may also have used a different material for roofing. In Chapter Three we saw that there was evidence for the earlier villa having a ceramic tile roof. In the third and fourth century there was a move away from the use of ceramic tiles to ones made from sandstone or limestone (Figure 41). These are usually hexagonal (six-sided) in shape and numerous fragments were found during the excavations.

Missing from the late Roman villa plan are any structures which could be identified as having an agricultural function, such as barns, granaries and work halls. Such buildings would have been central to the day to day management of a large estate. If the villa is proved to extend further to the south, these structures may form part of an outermost court or alternatively, they may be to one side so as not to impinge on the grand visual aspect the villa will have presented to

41 Reconstructed section of a late Roman stone tile roof

approaching visitors.

Beyond the west, north and east ranges which form the core of the villa, fragmentary but extensive remains of further rooms are known to the east and west. On the east rooms 18, 19, 20, 42 and 53 form a further range traced for a distance of over 25 metres (82 feet). Two rooms, 18 and 20, had mosaic floors. The example in room 18 was fragmentary and the design is lost. The floor in room 20 was in a much better state of preservation and featured a geometric pattern (Figure 42). A further mosaic may have existed in room 53.

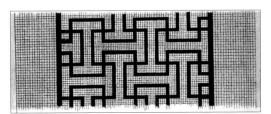

42 Part of the pattern of the mosaic floor in Room 20 as recorded by Sir Harold Brakspear

The wall dividing rooms 18 and 20 was 1.22 metres (4 feet) thick and suggests it was a major load bearing feature.

A very large and well-constructed drain passes below this range and was clearly intended to deal with large quantities of water. The source and destination of the drain remain unknown but small-scale investigations in the garden of The Vicarage have uncovered a number of additional Roman walls on a variety of alignments. It is clear that there is a further large range in this area but the character and function must remain unknown for now. Below the Selwyn Hall a further Roman wall and a ditch have been recorded but the wall is slight in character and unlikely to be from a load bearing or substantial structure. It is thought that these features may be part of a formal garden.

Roman Remains to the East and West of the Villa House

THE REMAINS TO the east of the villa are fragmentary and difficult to characterise, although it is possible that these will eventually prove to be part of the agricultural ranges so far missing from the plan.

A more extensive range of structures runs to the west of the main villa and into the grounds of Box House (Figure 43). Well-built and substantial walls on a common alignment with the villa have been found at The Wilderness, below Church Lane, Box House Cottage and Box House. These indicate a range up to 80 metres (262 feet) in length and include at least one heated room and a very substantial stone-built drain. Additional traces of Roman walling and a possible hypocaust have also been recorded

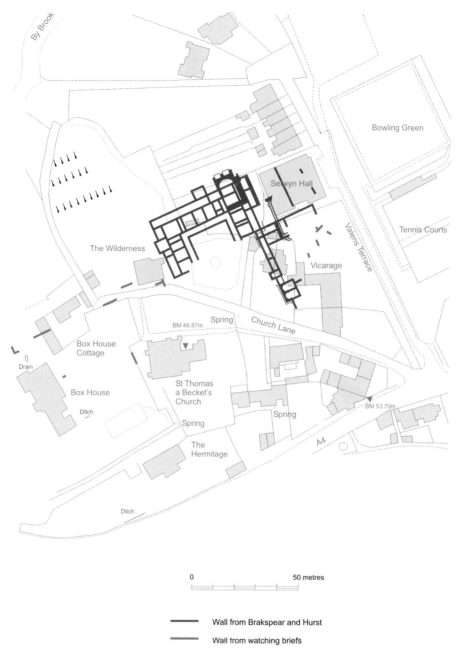

Bowling Green

Selwyn Hall

Tennis Courts

Valens Terrace

The Wilderness

Vicarage

Spring

Church Lane

BM 46.87m

Box House
Cottage

Drain

Box House

St Thomas
a Becket's
Church

Spring

BM 53.70m

Ditch

Spring

Spring

The
Hermitage

A4

Ditch

0   50 metres

——— Wall from Brakspear and Hurst

——— Wall from watching briefs

43 All recorded walls and other features adjacent to the villa

immediately to the east of Box House and suggest that further structures
may continue beneath the site of the present house.

The evidence of ranges to the east and west of the main villa poses

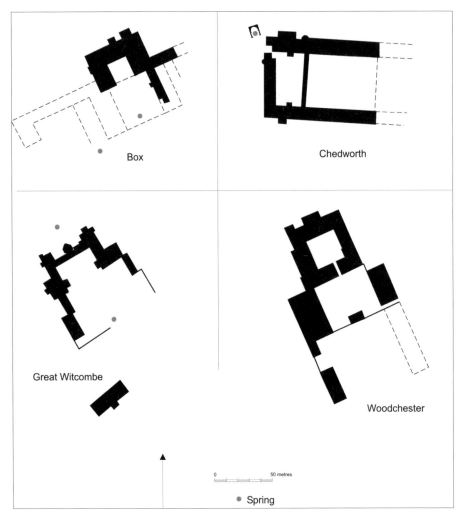

44 *Comparative block plans and other large villas in the region*

many questions, and the extent of the known remains shows the scale of the site as comparable with some of the largest villas known in western Roman Britain (Figure 44). The additional ranges at Box have few parallels in Roman Britain, especially that to the west, and may indicate this had a different function from the rest of the villa.

The springs adjacent to the tufa terrace on which the villa was constructed provide a reliable and copious supply of water. These would have had a strong attraction to the local population as more than a mere water supply. Three springs still flow today, all rising in the vicinity of the present church. The association between springs and religious sites, especially with healing cults, has origins in prehistory and continued into the Roman period and beyond; the veneration of the hot springs in Bath being an obvious and local example. This association suggests a further possible function for the Box villa as a place of worship, healing and pilgrimage. A potential location for this activity would be the range to the west of the villa where the topography allows for a large level area to be enclosed adjacent to a spring rising south of the church. Towards the southern side of this area is The Hermitage where the ditch excavated in 1982 produced much building rubble, pottery and a life-size eye made of silver, possibly a votive object associated with healing (eye complaints are known to have been very common in the Roman world). In addition to the eye, pieces of sculpture from the Box villa also point to a religious focus on the site. Part of a relief depicting a hunter god found in room 23 has already been mentioned (Figure 34). To this we may add a further piece, part of a relief depicting a hand holding a trident, possibly a representation of Neptune or related water deity, recorded as being 'probably found' in the grounds of Box House (Figure 45). If the find spot is correct then it is tempting to suggest that the sculpture came from a religious monument near to one of the springs. A stone capital in the Ionic order, also probably found at Box House, may have come from such a monument.

45 *Relief showing a hand holding a trident, possibly from a relief depicting Neptune, probably from the grounds of Box House (Cunliffe and Fulford 1982, plate 29, no. 110)*

Other villa sites in the region have also been interpreted as having a religious function, notably Chedworth and Great Witcombe, both associated with springs. At Chedworth a large shrine or Nymphaeum was built around the main spring feeding the complex, and the villa is overlooked by a large structure, probably a temple and mausoleum.

The presence of springs, sculpture with a religious theme and the silver eye from Box makes the proposal of a religious function an attractive one. This would be in addition to the villa functioning as a great estate centre.

Religious sites were widespread in the Roman world and took many forms, ranging from large urban complexes such as Bath, small rural shrines serving local communities and larger rural sanctuaries where worshippers had a wide range of facilities on offer. There is sufficient evidence to propose

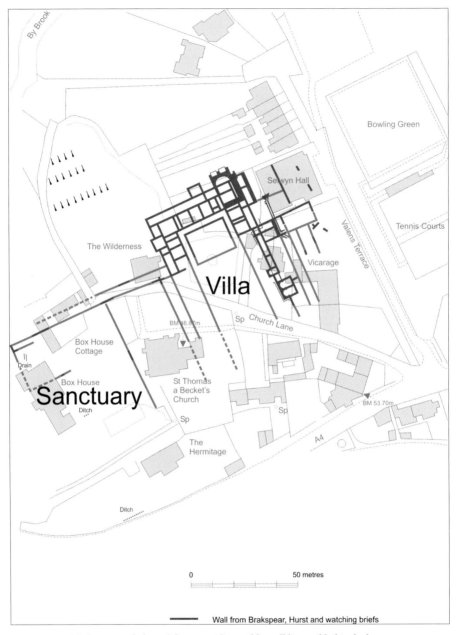

46 *Conjectural plan of the site with possible wall lines added in dark grey*

that Box may fall into the latter category. In addition to offering a place of worship, rural sanctuaries could also feature other facilities including bathing establishments and accommodation. All of these features were available at Box. In western Britain a number of excavated examples are known including Lydney in the Forest of Dean, Pagan's Hill near Chew Magna and Nettleton near Castle Combe. Box could be reconstructed as a site with a dual function comprising a religious complex focussed around the area of Box House and a large villa to the east (Figure 46). The two functions need not be mutually exclusive. If the Box springs were regarded as having curative powers, the proximity of the site to Bath would have provided a rural and tranquil alternative to the urban complex and perhaps attract wealthier worshippers. A religious sanctuary would have provided an additional source of income and may partly account for the large number of mosaic floors. It is quite possible that one or more ranges of the villa could also have provided accommodation for the wealthier visitors to the site.

By the middle of the fourth century AD the site at Box will have become the largest known villa complex in the Bath region, possibly the southern Cotswolds. The remains as currently known show it to have been a very richly appointed villa estate centre with an additional function as a religious sanctuary, perhaps a rural healing centre. Clearly much still remains to be discovered in the area and this is addressed in Chapter Nine. Attention is now turned to what daily life would have been like for those who owned the complex and the people dependent upon it.

5

The Romano-British Landscape and Economy of the Box Area

WE HAVE ALREADY seen that much of the landscape of Britain, covered by extensive field systems, had been established during the pre-Roman conquest period. These fields were maintained, sometimes modified and frequently extended during the Roman period. The pre-Roman farming communities were clearly capable of producing a large surplus of cereals and many Iron Age farms and hillforts were dominated by deep pits used as underground grain silos. Grain formed the basis of the wealth of many pre-Roman communities and will have been an important economic factor in the Roman scheme for the development of the province. The landscape of Roman Britain was densely settled and there was pressure to increase yields. In some areas around the coast of Britain we can identify extensive areas of Roman drainage and land reclamation to increase areas of arable and pasture. This is most clearly seen around the Fens of East Anglia and on either side of the Severn Estuary in Gloucestershire, Somerset and Gwent. In some parts of the country an integrated pattern of villages, farms and villas is common although many regional variations are evident. As with many of the field systems it can be demonstrated that a number of rural settlements have origins pre-dating the Roman conquest and these frequently expanded as the Romano-British economy grows. The settlement pattern was especially dense in the south of the country with large concentrations of villas and their dependent farms clustering around many of the urban centres. The towns will have provided administrative, market and cultural facilities for the rural population. In the south-west of Britain there were notable clusters of villas around the towns of Cirencester, Bath and Ilchester with the Cotswold Hills and environs having one of the highest densities of villas known in Roman Britain (Figure 47). In other parts of the region, such as on Salisbury Plain where there are no major Roman towns, recent work has identified villages covering areas as large as 20 hectares (50 acres), larger than the walled area of Roman Bath. The majority of the villages reached their maximum extent during the fourth century AD with evidence for a heavy emphasis

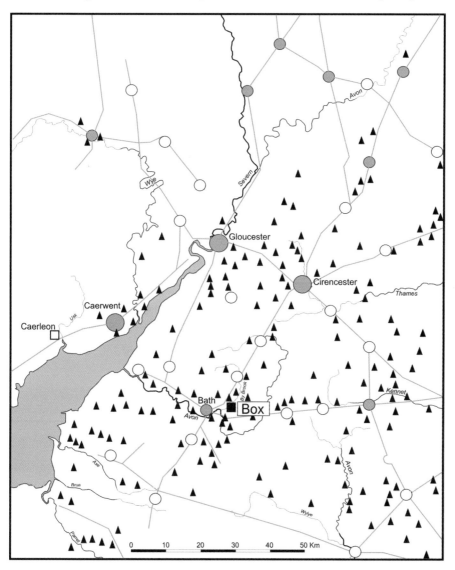

47 *Roman roads, towns and villas in the region. The black triangles represent known villas*

48 A lead ingot found on Mendip. It carries an inscription bearing the name of the Emperor Vespasian who ruled between AD69 and AD79

on cereal production. These are most likely to have been 'estate villages' dependent upon parent villas distributed around the edge of Salisbury Plain and the valley of the River Avon. The cumulative evidence provided by air photography, geophysics and modern excavation coupled with antiquarian records and stray finds, all provide an impression of a landscape geared towards intensive levels of agricultural production.

Although a predominantly agrarian society and landscape, farming would have been supplemented by localised industries. In the west of Britain these ranged from pottery production to metalworking and stone quarrying. The large-scale exploitation of iron deposits is known in the Forest of Dean, Gloucestershire and from Westbury in Wiltshire; lead was mined (and silver extracted from the ore) at a number of sites on the Mendip Hills. At Charterhouse-on-Mendip there are still extensive surface remains of Roman mining, the associated settlement and a possible amphitheatre (Figure 48).

Using Mendip lead (and tin from Cornwall), a number of pewter manufacturing workshops are known in and around Bath with stone moulds for casting vessels recorded from settlements at Westbury in Wiltshire, Camerton near Radstock and on Lansdown (Figure 49).

Large numbers of pewter vessels have been discovered in the Sacred Spring to Sulis-Minerva at Bath and were clearly popular as votive offerings to the Goddess. Mendip lead was used to line the base of the Great Bath in *Aquae Sulis* (Bath) and was also widely used in the plumbing of public and private buildings across southern Britain. The

49 Part of a limestone mould for casting vessel components in pewter. Found in Bath

manufacture of day to day utilitarian pottery occurred locally and from the third century AD more specialised and higher quality table wares were made near Oxford and the New Forest, largely replacing the continental products imported in large numbers in the first and second centuries AD. The high-quality limestone of the Bath area was a highly prized stone and occurs widely over southern Britain being used both as a building material and for sculpture. In the Bristol region the distinctive purple-red pennant sandstone was widely quarried in the Roman period and used as roof tiles, usually of hexagonal shape. Numerous fragments of such tiles are known from Box and other sites around Bath.

The period of greatest prosperity for the province of Britannia was from about 250AD until the end of the fourth century, and this is most clearly reflected in the countryside. There are a number of reasons for this. By the middle of the third century AD the Roman-British economy had matured with the potential for the accumulation of surplus capital which could be invested in well-constructed houses. As a consequence stone villas began to appear in considerable numbers across the landscape from this date. Some were developments of existing farms and earlier country homes whilst others appear to have been built anew. The political and economic character of the Roman Empire was also changing during this period. Political uncertainty and frequent rebellions and civil wars put the Empire under considerable strain and between 260AD and 274AD Britain joined with Spain and Gaul to form the breakaway Gallic Empire with the capital at Cologne on the River Rhine. This event will have put Britain in an important position as a producer of grain. The large number of inscribed milestones of this date found in Britain show that the regime was actively repairing and investing in the transport infrastructure of the province. The mainland of Europe was also beginning to suffer from major raids by Germanic tribes from east of the River Rhine. The effects of these were especially felt in Gaul (modern France and Belgium) with widespread disruption to the rural economy and destruction of property. Raids and occasional full invasions continued after the reunification of the Empire in 274AD. By the end of the third century AD the security situation had improved and the Roman state was exercising a stronger and more centralised control of the economy. The emperor Diocletian issued an edict fixing the price of many commodities. British items feature on this edict and include beer, priced at a higher tariff than its Gallic counterpart and a quality woollen garment called the Birrus Britannicus. This was a short woollen cloak with a hood and is shown on a figure depicting winter on a mosaic floor from the villa at Chedworth near Cirencester (Figure 50).

50 Detail of a mosaic from the Chedworth Roman villa showing the personification of Winter gathering sticks for fuel. The figure is wearing a short, hooded cloak known as the Birrus Britannicus

Wool and textile production will also have been very important to the late Roman economy of Britain, and a late fourth century AD document names an Imperial textile mill in Britain at a place identified as *Venta*. Three towns are known by this name; Winchester, Caistor-by-Norwich and Caerwent in south Wales. All are possible candidates, being in areas where wool production continued to be important in the post-Roman period.

Britain appears to have been largely spared the trauma of regular raiding. There is little convincing archaeological evidence for raiding or destruction during this period and our island location probably acted as a protection. From about 280AD onwards a chain of forts were constructed around the south-east coastline of Britain and are known as the 'Forts of the Saxon Shore'. Once thought to be a chain of coastal defence bases, their distribution and wide spacing argues against this being a primary function. It is now thought that they were fortified collection points for the gathering of grain and other commodities from the interior of Britain and claimed by the Roman state as a tax-in-kind known as the *annona militaris*. From these bases the produce could be graded and shipped directly to Gaul and the Rhine frontier to support the garrisons based there. It is recorded that large quantities of British grain were shipped across the English Channel in 358-9AD to alleviate the effects of famine caused by midwinter barbarian raids into Gaul. There is undoubtedly a correlation between the growth of wealthy villas and other settlements in the Romano-British countryside and the deteriorating economic and political fortunes of the later Roman Empire. The boom in British villa building with their high quality features such as mosaics, painted walls and the obvious material wealth has led some to call the fourth century AD 'The Golden Age of Roman Britain'.

In western Britain there is little doubt that the fourth century AD saw major developments of villas, rural settlements and renewed building in towns. This is reflected very clearly in the Roman archaeology of the Box region.

The Box villa is located approximately 8km to the east of the major Roman religious and civil centre of *Aquæ Sulis*, modern Bath. In addition to the extensive Roman spa and religious complex, Bath will have also acted as the local administrative and market centre for the surrounding countryside. The regional capital, Cirencester, was too distant for everyday needs, although specialist services such as mosaicists would probably have been based there. Box is situated close to two major Roman roads; the Fosse Way, linking Bath to Cirencester is 2.5km to the west, and 2km to the south is the road from Silchester to Bath, the line of which still survives as the modern parish boundary between Box, Monkton Farleigh, South Wraxall and Atworth. A link from the major Roman road network to the villa must have existed but its location remains unknown; the topography of the area would strongly suggest that at least one route would have approached from the south-east, possibly following the line of the modern A361. A further direct link towards Bath may be anticipated, perhaps close to the line of the present A4 west of Box.

The limestone plateau to the south of Box has extensive traces of field systems integrated with ditched trackways of later prehistoric and Romano-British date. These are known from air photography and as surviving earthworks which can be traced as far south as the Roman villa recently discovered at St Laurence's School, Bradford on Avon. Especially well preserved remains of fields and tracks of Iron Age origin and used throughout the Roman period survive at Inwood to the south of Bathford. The area around Box has produced numerous finds of Romano-British material, suggesting an ordered and relatively open landscape with scattered villas, farms and other settlements. A detailed consideration of these sites is included here to illustrate the diversity and density of substantial Romano-British buildings labelled as villas in the region. Doubtless others still await discovery.

There are at least ten villas, or probable villas, within a 5km radius of Box and these are part of a more extensive distribution of well-appointed villas which cluster around Bath. To the north of the By Brook at least four villas are known. In Colerne parish, at ST811718, a villa probably built around a central hall with a bath suite on the west side was first discovered in 1838 and investigated further in 1854. The villa plan (Figure 51) includes a bipartite or double room with a polygonal apse. This room was heated by a hypocaust and had a mosaic floor. The latter had been largely destroyed by the time of discovery and no details survive. A further three mosaics are recorded, one of which may have included a depiction of a *quadriga* (four horsed chariot used in racing) and the name SERVIVS or SEVERVS. Depictions of chariots are rare in Roman Britain and this floor may well have been a special commission by the villa owner; perhaps a fan of this popular Roman sport. The name picked out on the mosaic may even be that of a champion charioteer. Little dating evidence is recorded other than 'Constantinian' coins of the first half of the fourth century AD, and a similar date is given to the mosaics on stylistic grounds by Stephen Cosh and David Neal in their masterly book on the Roman Mosaics in Britain.

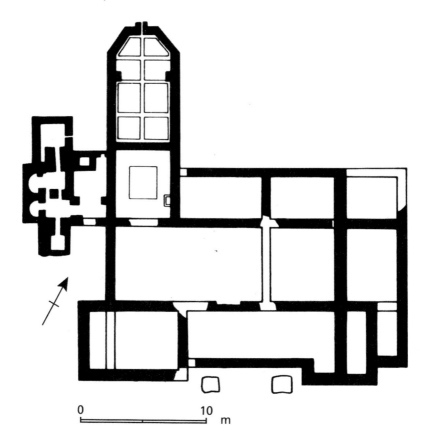

51 Plan of the Colerne villa (After Cosh & Neal, 2005).

The listings of archaeological records maintained as a legal planning requirement by Wiltshire Council (known as the Wiltshire Historic Environment Record or HER) has a record of two lengths of wall, painted wall plaster, five Constantinian coins, pottery, tiles, Samian and New Forest pottery sherds, and a piece of sculpture from the west of the By Brook in the grounds of Colerne Park, ST836729. These would strongly suggest the presence of a substantial building, possibly a villa, but further details are lacking.

To the south of Euridge Manor Farm, ST ST833716 is a south-facing villa of corridor plan with numerous outbuildings covering an area of about 2ha. The site overlooks a minor tributary of the By Brook and has produced ceramic flue tiles, roof tiles, much pottery, coins and metalwork from the 1st to 4th centuries and part of a sculpture depicting Hercules slaying the Hydra. The majority of the datable objects are of fourth century date. A geophysical survey undertaken in 1998 revealed details of the villa layout with the probable

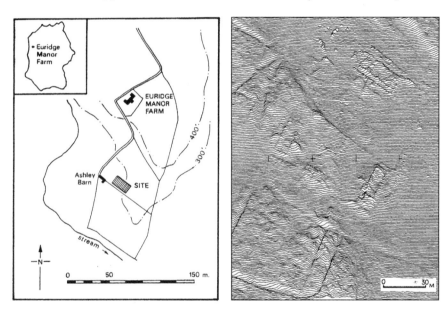

52 *Location and geophysical survey of the villa south of Euridge Manor Farm (Luckett et al, 2000)*

main range to the north with a pair of ranges to the west and east defining an inner court and a possible gate-house on the south side. There is an outer court beyond with a further range along the east side. Traces of probable ditched tracks and field boundaries can also be discerned (Figure 52).

The Wiltshire Historic Environment Record records a probable villa at Ditteridge, ST816694, discovered in 1813, but few details are known and further fieldwork is desirable to confirm this antiquarian observation.

South of the By Brook further villas are known. Approximately 1km to the east of Box a mosaic, now lost, was reported as being found before 1719 near to Hazelbury Manor. A contemporary account records the mosaic as within a building reported as being 45m in length (Figure 53). An air photograph taken in 1973 and published by Henry Hurst in his 1989 report of the Box villa shows a rectangular ditched enclosure to the south of Hazelbury Manor which may indicate the approximate position of the discovery. There are also anecdotal accounts of Roman remains being found in this area during the 1930s. In their book on the Roman mosaics in Britain the authors, Stephen Cosh and David Neal, query whether this discovery is in fact a mis-located antiquarian reference to an early discovery of part of the Box villa. Only further field work can resolve this question.

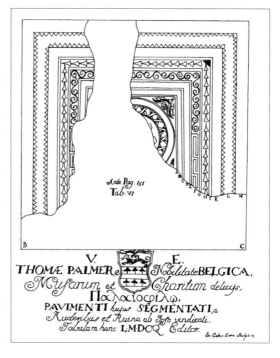

53 *Engraving by Coles of the Hazelbury Manor mosaic (from Cosh and Neal, 2005, figure 369)*

Three km to the south-east of Box and to the south of the Roman road from Silchester to Bath is the villa at Atworth. Initially excavated immediately before the Second World War by A.T. Shaw Mellor, a former Box resident, and again in the early 1970s, the plan is of a south facing house with an east range which includes a bath suite at the southernmost end. A large detached aisled building, probably a barn and work hall, lies opposite the east range (Figure 54). Although now badly damaged by ploughing, the villa was clearly well appointed and topsoil finds of fine tesserae indicate the former presence of mosaic floors. The finds suggest occupation between the second and fourth centuries with the main structural periods falling into the latter part of this date range. The discovery of a large number of industrial structures within the main house, east range and detached aisled building, and generally interpreted as either grain-dryers or malting kilns, strongly suggests that this site was the centre of a large estate engaged in cereal production and processing. The 1970s excavations also recovered some evidence to suggest that the site continued in use into the fifth century AD, beyond the supposed end of Roman rule.

Three km to the west of Atworth, south of Box and west of Norbin Barton Farm at ST819661, extensive surface scatters of building materials and pottery are suggestive of another villa sited, like Atworth, just to the south of the road from Silchester to Bath. This is within an area where air photographs show extensive traces of a regular field system and appears to be part of the same landscape which survives as earthworks further west at Inwood.

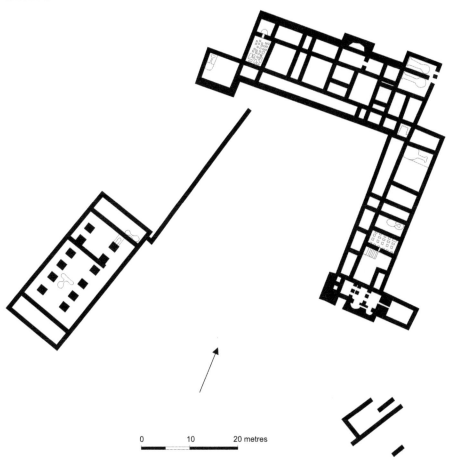

54 Plan of the villa at Atworth (After Erskine & Ellis 2008).

To the south-west of Box a further two villas are recorded at Bathford; both known only from early antiquarian records and there is little detailed information. The first site was found in 1691 or 1692 in a field called Horselands, located between Bathford church and the River Avon, approximately 100 yards below Low House. The discovery is said to have included a pavement 14 feet square, supported by a pillared hypocaust which, in its turn, seems to have stood on an earlier mosaic floor suggesting a complex structural sequence. The seventeenth-century biographer and antiquarian John Aubrey also records the discovery of a mosaic at Bathford in May 1655. He says, 'it was worked in the usual white (chalk), blue (lias) and red (brick): in the centre was a rudely figured bird and in each of the four corners a sort of knot.' Below it was a hypocaust with stone pillars and also a spring of water. The presence of mosaics and a hypocaust leaves little doubt that this is a villa site. A second possible villa near Bathford is recorded at Mumford's or Mompas Mead, between Bathford village and Warleigh, close to the east bank of the River Avon. This site has produced an elaborate square pilaster capital of the Composite order, now stored in The Roman Baths Museum, as well as a stone coffin and tiles. The site today is visible as a low, stony mound and from time to time pieces of pennant sandstone roof tiles, typical of later Roman roofing material, can be seen on the surface.

At Hollies Lane on the eastern flank of Charmy Down (ST776691), 4.5km to the north-west of Box, excavations in 1990 and 1991 by the Bath Archaeological Trust investigated a villa of winged corridor plan with walls surviving up to 1.9m high, some still retaining painted wall plaster. Further structures, including a stone water cistern, have also been recorded. The finds suggest a fourth-century date.

Somewhat further away from the examples described above but worthy of mention is the Roman villa complex investigated below the playing fields of St Laurence School at Bradford on Avon between 2002 and 2004. In 1976 part of a bath-suite had been discovered and partly excavated on the edge of the school property. At this time it was thought that the remains were part of a villa which had been largely destroyed by an adjacent housing estate. During a spell of hot weather in 1999 the outline of a series of stone buildings was noted as yellow lines in the drought-stricken grass of the playing field, and subsequent geophysical survey revealed the plan of a large villa complex (Figure 55). The two largest buildings are of what is called a 'winged corridor' type and share a common alignment with near identical plans and dimensions. Excavation demonstrated that both were initially constructed in the mid- to late-third century AD although there had been earlier Roman activity on the site. Despite the similarity in plan, their functions were found to be very different. The eastern building is a well-appointed house with a near intact mosaic floor surviving in the central main chamber (Figure 55). The building

10   0   50   100 Metres

55 Plan of the villa at St Laurence School, Bradford on Avon. Building 1 is the main house; building 2 an agri-industrial structure mimicking the villa house; building 4 includes the bath-suite excavated in1976. The other buildings are known only from air photography or geophysics and their function remains unknown.

also had painted plaster walls and the numerous fragments of window glass show it was glazed. The baths excavated in 1976 are now known to be in the west range of this building. The second winged corridor building, although resembling a large house externally, appears to have been given over to agri-industrial activities with grain drying, metalworking and a possible smoke house for curing foodstuffs. Externally it would have appeared much like the neighbouring house and this is almost certainly a deliberate architectural device to impress visitors with a double façade on the main approach to the site. In the early-fifth century AD part of the main house was adapted and what appears to be a Christian baptistery was constructed within the central room. This comprised the construction of a circular stone platform over part of the mosaic. It had a central depression, possibly for the font, and an adjacent deep soakaway pit (Figure 56). The Bradford an Avon site is important because it is one of the very few so far identified in the region where the very latest archaeological levels have survived. This survival allowed the early post-Roman period to be investigated and sheds light on the fate of the villa following the decline of Roman rule and the collapse of the centralised economy. These important levels were removed without record at Box during the nineteenth-century excavations.

56 Vertical view of the central bi-partite room of the main house at the Bradford on Avon villa showing the well-preserved mosaic floor as exposed in 2003. The circular feature overlying the mosaic floor to the right of centre is thought to be the base of a Christian baptistery dating to the fifth century AD.

Although all of the sites described above are undoubtedly villas which provided comfortable homes and were probably based on estates, none is close to Box in terms of scale and the number of mosaics. This reinforces the impression that the Box villa is an exceptional site in the local rural settlement hierarchy. It is even possible that some of the neighbouring sites may have been part of the Box villa estate and had been sub-let to tenants.

In addition to the villas, the majority of which would have represented the country houses of the wealthier classes, villages and smaller farms were a common feature of the landscape. Surprisingly few examples of this type of site have been located with certainty in the immediate environs of Box although they must exist. The remains of this class of settlement are less substantial than villas and, generally lacking mosaic floors, bath-houses and rich finds, will not have been so obvious to early antiquarians. The discovery of such sites remains a challenge for local fieldworkers.

In the wider Bath environs a number of other settlements are known. At the northern end of Lansdown, north of Bath and close to the Civil War monument erected to Sir Bevil Grenville, there are extensive earthwork remains of a Romano-British village. Covering at least 2 hectares (5 acres), excavation in the early-twentieth century uncovered simple stone buildings, paved surfaces and moulds for producing pewter vessels. The majority of the finds date to the third and fourth century AD. This may have been a largely agricultural settlement with a 'cottage industry' producing pewter vessels which were sold to pilgrims and worshippers in Bath to supplement income. Further small village-type settlements of Roman date also survive as earthworks on the plateaux of Charmy Down and Bathampton Down, but very few have been investigated in detail.

Roadside settlements astride the Roman roads leading out of Bath are known at a number of locations. These sites will have provided a number of functions ranging from a local marketing and manufacturing centre to more specialised activities such as shrines and temples.

An especially large site is known at Camerton, north of Radstock laid out on either side of the Fosse Way (Figure 57). Like Box, the Camerton site was first investigated in the nineteenth century, in this case by a well known local antiquarian and cleric, the Reverend John Skinner. A settlement had already been established here in the Iron Age and in 1980 a large hoard of decorated late Iron Age and early Roman metalwork was found and is now in the British Museum. The character of the hoard, including early Roman military items may even point to an as yet undiscovered fort of the conquest period close by. The construction of the Fosse Way in the first century AD would have given the Iron Age settlement a new impetus. An excavation between 1926 and 1956 revealed the plans of a number of structures. The majority of the buildings were of a simple 'strip' plan and represented shops or workshops, probably with accommodation to the rear. These were mainly located along the Fosse Way frontage and are typical of commercial properties known across the Roman world. Set back from the Fosse Way were two larger buildings of more complex plan similar in appearance to a villa. Although the excavations have only investigated part of the site, there is some evidence to suggest that the settlement even had a partly planned street layout although the alignments differ on either side of the Fosse Way. One building produced stone moulds for the casting of pewter vessels.

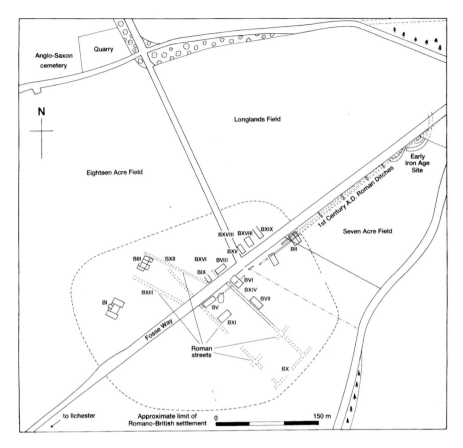

57 Plan of the Roman roadside settlement at Camerton, north of Radstock. Note the simple plan of the majority of the excavated buildings

To the north of Bath there are two large settlements known along the route of the Fosse Way. These are fairly evenly spaced between Bath and Cirencester and developed where the road crossed rivers. The northernmost is located near Easton Grey to the west of Malmesbury where the Fosse Way crosses the River Avon. There has been very little modern investigation here and the history of the site remains unknown. The second and more extensively explored site is at Nettleton, near Castle Combe.

Set beside the Fosse Way where it crosses a tributary of the By Brook and some 10km north of Box, Nettleton is a most remarkable and interesting site. Excavations between 1938 and 1947 and again from 1956 to 1970 investigated an extensive roadside settlement which appears to be largely religious in character. In the Roman period a stream, the Broadmead Brook, was canalised and a large group of stone structures built along the south bank (Figure 58). The most notable of these was an octagonal structure set on a massive stone-built platform and serving as a temple. Sculpture and votive offerings show that a number of deities were venerated here including Silvanus (a protector of the woods often associated with hunting) and Mercury. Mercury in the north-western provinces was often associated with commerce and was the protector of merchants. The principle deity however appears to have been Apollo Cunomaglos – a local amalgamation of the classical god Apollo and the north-western European

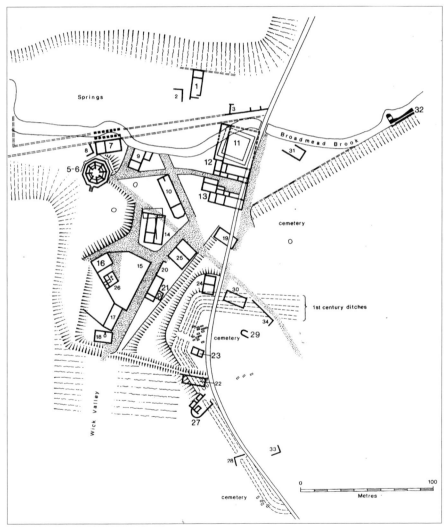

58 Plan of the Roman temple and settlement complex on the Fosse Way at Nettleton near Castle Combe. Building 5-6 is the temple, 11-13 the probable guesthouse and 32 a water-mill

god 'Cunomaglos', which roughly translates as 'Hound-prince' This deity is also attested at a temple on Pagan's Hill near Chewton Mendip and he may have been an important local pre-Roman god. In addition to associations with the underworld, Apollo and his local equivalents had strong healing attributes. At Nettleton there were numerous other buildings in addition to the temple, including one which was deliberately built across the Broadmead Brook and is thought to have been used for ritual bathing, cleansing and healing. A large courtyard building, probably a guest-house for pilgrims, was built on to the Fosse Way frontage and there were strip buildings used as workshops, including one, as at Camerton, with evidence for the manufacture of pewter vessels. The Nettleton complex is one of the finest examples of a Romano-British rural shrine dedicated to a range of local and Roman deities. The provision of accommodation and supporting facilities shows that this was a place of pilgrimage. Nettleton is easily within a day's travelling distance of Box during the Roman period and the residents of the villa may have worshipped here from time to time. The site would have provided a more rural and tranquil alternative to the busy and cosmopolitan religious attractions of Bath.

A more secular aspect to the site is also indicated by the remains of a Roman water-mill on the banks of the Broadmead Brook at the eastern edge of the site. Late Roman modifications to the octagonal temple led the excavator to suggest that in its final form the building may have been converted into a church, although absolute proof is lacking. An extensive late Roman cemetery may also be Christian in character and this continued in use into the fifth century AD or even later.

Sites such as Nettleton clearly illustrate that Roman religion was not confined to the larger urban centres. Rural places of worship, ranging from large complexes such as Nettleton to simple rural shrines were common in the landscape and show that the people of the pagan Roman world held a deep and diverse range of religious beliefs.

Other roadside or rural shrines will have been present in the region. To the east of Atworth, along the line of the Roman road from London to Bath, a large number of Roman brooches and a late Roman gold buckle found in fields near Gastard may indicate the site of a roadside shrine or temple. Brooches were an especially common votive offering at many rural shrines.

Stray finds can also be informative and hint at specialised activities. Found only 600m to the south-east of the Box villa was a crude carved limestone head of so called 'Romano-Celtic' type (Figure 59). The head features prominent ears, lentoid eyes and simply depicted mouth and nose.

This was found in the grounds of 'Sunny View Cottage' in Henley Lane, Box and is now held in Devizes Museum. Carved heads of this form are relatively widespread across Roman Britain and are clearly deliberately crude and naïve in execution. They tend to be mainly rural finds and it has been suggested that they are a manifestation of the continuation of head cults which had origins in the pre-Roman period. As this was a surface find we cannot be certain whether it had lain at the place of discovery since the Roman period or whether it may have been introduced from elsewhere. It may even have originally come from the villa site where there is a possibility of a religious function.

Elsewhere in the area occasional stray finds of Roman pottery and other objects may have many origins. Some could indicate hitherto unrecognised occupation sites or, alternatively, simply be derived from domestic rubbish from known sites and mixed with manure to be spread on the Roman fields.

59 'Romano-Celtic' stone head from
Sunny View Cottage, Henley Lane, Box

6
Life on the Villa

A T THIS POINT we digress from the narrative to become somewhat more speculative, and attempt to reconstruct what life would have been like for those who owned, lived and worked at the villa in the opening decades of the fourth century AD. There are very few historical sources from the Roman period which will give us detailed information on day-to-day life. What accounts we do have are primarily concerned with praising the Emperor, his family and his achievements; what we would call propaganda. It is principally the archaeological evidence, coupled with the few historical sources, which provide the basis for this chapter. We know that the period was one of stability and, for the province of Britannia Prima, one of prosperity. Now under the rule of the Emperor Constantine and his sons, Britain had not long emerged from a period of active participation in rebellion.

The majority of villas across the empire derived their wealth from farming, Britain being no exception. Agriculture in the Roman world was highly labour intensive and the bulk of the population will have been engaged in working the land. The workforce were most likely a mix of slaves coupled with a peasant class; the latter increasingly tied to the estates and their owners. The larger estates may also have owned further villas which would have been let to tenants or managed by a bailiff. During the Roman period new types of higher yielding cereals were introduced to Britain, notably bread wheat which was being cultivated alongside other varieties such as spelt and emmer. Other established cereals such as oats, barley and rye continued to be grown. We have already seen that there is very good evidence for extensive field systems and an ordered landscape across much of Roman Britain. These fields would have been used to raise livestock and grow cereals. Domesticated species were very similar to those farmed today although somewhat smaller in size. In the case of Box, with the local availability of good quality building stone, quarrying could have provided an additional source of income.

Technological innovation in the Roman world was minimal, although the demand by the state for foodstuffs and other products led to a greater and more efficient organisation of the labour force, landscape and administration. The fields would have been cultivated using ox teams pulling a simple plough known as an ard (Figure 60) and the harvest undertaken largely by hand using sickles. There is evidence that a simple form of reaping machine or harvester was used in Roman Gaul, modern France and Belgium. Known as the *vallus*, this machine is depicted on a number of sculptures and was pushed by a mule (Figure 61). Although we do not have any direct evidence for the use of this machine in Roman Britain it is quite possible, if

60 *Replica of a Roman plough*

not probable, that many of the larger estates in this country will have used it. Wheat was a very important cereal crop in late Roman Britain and we have already seen that Britain was able to supply other parts of the Empire in times of famine and stress. The presence of malting kilns at many villas and rural settlements may also indicate that much of the barley produced was used for brewing.

At large villas such as Box the day to day running of the estate would have been left in the hands of an estate manager or bailiff, allowing the villa owner to pursue other activities. These would include his local government obligations, the receiving and entertaining of local dignitaries, provincial officials and leisure pursuits such as hunting. The

61 *Relief from Buzenol in modern Belgium showing a reaping machine called the vallus*

62 Part of a mosaic from East Coker in Somerset depicting hunters returning with a deer. A scene such as this will have been common at Box. This floor is now on display in the Somerset County Museum in Taunton

surrounding landscape would have been rich with game, including deer and wild boar. Hunting was a favourite pursuit for the wealthy classes in the Roman world and depictions of the hunt are a common theme for mosaic floors across the empire. A fine example of a mosaic floor depicting hunters returning with a deer comes from East Coker in Somerset (Figure 62) and is a scene which will have been very familiar to the owner of Box and other villas across Roman Britain.

The daily routine for the owner and his family would vary according to their commitments. For the children of the owner the mornings were most probably spent at lessons (Figure 63). They would expect to commence formal education at about the age of six and continue until they were thirteen or fourteen. This usually included all children irrespective of sex and they will have received sufficient education to be literate. The wealthier classes had a private household tutor, possibly a slave who might be fluent in Greek as well as Latin. In addition to basic literacy the child would have learnt mathematics, Greek and Roman classics, grammar, poetry, oratory and rhetoric; the latter two being considered important skills for anyone where public service was destined to play an important part in adult life.

Basic literacy in later Roman Britain must have been widespread, based upon the evidence of graffiti on pot sherds, and the level of education amongst the wealthy classes would have been considerably higher. It is very likely that the level of literacy in later Roman Britain would not be achieved again until the nineteenth century.

63 A relief depicting a Roman schoolmaster and his pupils. The schoolmaster is seated in the centre with pupils either side; the boy on the far right is arriving late for lessons and no doubt like countless generations since has an implausible excuse ready!

Education in the classics was essential for the wealthy and aristocratic classes, and knowledge of classical mythology and the pagan pantheon by villa owners is evident from the numerous depictions of these themes found on mosaic floors in Britain. At the Lullingstone villa in Kent a magnificent fourth-century AD mosaic depicts the abduction of Europa by Jupiter and includes a quotation from the Roman author Virgil. In western Britain floors showing scenes of Orpheus charming wild beasts by playing the lyre are popular in a number of very wealthy villas. It is tempting to speculate that a floor of similar quality and inspiration may have once adorned the great apsidal chamber at Box, room 26.

While the children were receiving tuition, the ladies of the household may have entertained guests and planned the menus for banquets being given for important guests. Wealthy women in the late Roman world also had much power and authority which extended beyond the household. If married, a woman of rank could still inherit and own property independently of her husband. We have already seen in Chapter Four that an aristocratic and wealthy lady named Melania is recorded as owning estates in Britain and other provinces in the late-fourth century AD, and that she eventually disposed of these to lead a life of Christian virtue.

If not away in Bath or Cirencester on business, during the morning the owner will have attended to the management of the estate, received petioners asking for favour and finance, dispensed justice and settled local disputes.

Other obligations of a great fourth-century AD landowner will have included ensuring that the tax in kind on estate produce was paid. Despite the unpopularity of this and other taxes the penalties for non-compliance could be draconian. These obligations to the state could also include the periodic supply of manpower for the army; the conscripts having to be equipped at the estate owners' expense. A visit from provincial financial officers would no doubt have been unwelcome, and contemporary accounts of the complaints from large landowners make it clear that many resented the high taxation burden. Despite these demands the levels of wealth were such that there would still be sufficient surplus cash to allow improvements to be made to the villa. During the first half of the fourth century AD many villa owners embarked on modifications and improvements including the laying of new mosaics or commissioning new wall paintings.

The owner of a villa on the scale of Box would have been an important client and patron for many local trades and services. The highly skilled craftsmen providing these services will have presented themselves with their pattern books from which the owner made his selections. The master mosaicist had probably travelled from Cirencester, the provincial capital and a known major centre of fine mosaic production in the fourth century. Other craftsmen, including metalsmiths, sculptors and architects, were probably based in Bath as well as Cirencester.

During the middle to later part of the day the villa owner may have gone to the bath-suite. This will often have been more than a mere act of personal hygiene, and bathing in the Roman world was often used as a social and business opportunity with guests or members of the family. Even though we do not know their full extent, the size of the east wing bath-suite at Box shows that it was admirably suited for such activities being decorated with painted walls and mosaic floors.

Roman bathing involved a number of prescribed stages. The bathers undressed in an ante-chamber and then proceeded through the cold room, perhaps pausing for an invigorating douche in the cold plunge, before moving on to the heated rooms. Here the bathers could relax, sip wine, chat and oil their bodies. Gambling may also have featured heavily. Dice are common finds on Roman sites in Britain and contemporary Roman writers noted that bathing and gambling often went hand in hand.

64 *A set of Roman bathing equipment from a villa in France. On the left is a pair of bronze instruments called a strigil used for scraping over the body, a bronze vessel for pouring water and, to the right, a glass flask which would have contained scented oil. The bathers at Box would each have owned a set very similar to these*

Each bather would have had their personal set of equipment to use. This would comprise a flask containing scented oil, a tool called a strigil for scraping the skin, and a small vessel for pouring water (Figure 64). Soap was not known in the Roman world, and as the bather began to sweat the pores opened with the dirt being drawn off the body and adhering to the oil. The bather would then use the strigil to scrape the oil and dirt off the body. The hot rooms of the bath-suite at Box housed a pair of plunge baths and here the bathers could wash off any remaining oil. The bathers could then indulge in a massage and return through the cold rooms to dress. In addition to the strigil and oil set, once into the hot rooms the bathers would have to wear thick wooden clogs to protect their feet from the heat of the hypocaust system. Examples of these have been found preserved in the waterlogged and oxygen-free levels of the Roman fort at Vindolanda on Hadrian's Wall.

To allow the villa owner, his family and guests to enjoy the bathing facility, a large number of slaves and household workers would have been required to work behind the scenes. To heat the hot rooms and plunge baths vast quantities of fuel would need to have been fed into the furnace. This will have been located in an adjacent service area, and working here must have been one of the dirtiest and most uncomfortable jobs in the house. Large quantities of fuel, probably charcoal, would have been stockpiled, and to maintain a constant temperature the furnace would require constant attention.

After the baths, the owner and guests may have taken a stroll around the formal gardens of the villa to appreciate the setting of the site. At Box this probably included a series of terraces between the north range of the villa and the By Brook. These may have included gravel paths flanked with shrubs such as box. There will also have been fruit trees and the garden would be adorned with statuary and perhaps small shrines. On the south side of the villa a series of courtyards probably surrounded further formal gardens, with each being flanked by a covered corridor allowing exercise to be taken during inclement weather. Later in the day, towards sunset, a formal dinner or banquet would be served.

At Box the north range of the villa has a number of rooms which could serve as a dining room. Room 6 will have been the summer family dining room and one of the heated rooms to either side, 5 and 7, will have been used in the winter. Room 29, overlooking the valley of the By Brook may also have been used as a more private summer dining room.

For larger formal dinners we can imagine that room 26 with the apse at the north end would be used. Here the lofty space with a backdrop of richly decorated walls and a mosaic floor would have been sufficient to accommodate a large number of diners. The owner and the most important guests no doubt occupied the apse and would have been the focus for other diners. This room will also have had adequate space to allow for entertainment which may have been provided by musicians, dancers and perhaps on occasion supplemented by poetry recitals. The diners would be arranged around tables and recline upon couches, to be served by personal servants or household slaves with a selection of dishes and fine wines (Figure 65).

At a villa on the scale of Box a banquet set in room 26 would have been presented on a service of silver. The workmanship and quality of fourth-century British silversmiths was very high and the service would be richly decorated with scenes from classical mythology. Examples of late Roman silver service from Britain can still be seen in the British Museum from Mildenhall and Hoxne, both in modern Suffolk. The surviving pieces from Hoxne included a fine silver gilt spice shaker, possibly for pepper. At this date pepper and most other spices was imported from India, and Britain was probably the most distant point reached by these valuable and highly prized commodities. Drink may have been consumed from either silver or glass vessels. In the fourth century very fine glass drinking cups were imported from the Rhineland of modern Germany with especially famed workshops being known around modern Cologne.

65 *An early 5th century* AD *illustration from a copy of the works of Virgil. The scene is of a formal dinner of the type that will have been held at Box in the 4th century. The diners are reclining on couches and are being served wine by servants. On the table the artist has shown fish and oysters; all foodstuffs that have been recorded from many villas in Roman Britain. The diners are shown with halos; these are originally an artistic device to indicate the rank of the individuals rather than a sign of sanctity*

The food served at banquets will have come from a variety of sources. Much of the meat would have been locally sourced, and archaeology shows that fowl (wild and domestic), beef, pork, venison and mutton were all consumed. These items would have been supplemented with foodstuffs from further afield, including fresh, dried and salted fish and British oysters, the latter being known for their quality and flavour. Vegetables included pulses such as lentils along with onions, garlic, peas, broad beans, carrots, radish, beetroot and cabbage. Sauces were herb or cheese based (the tomato yet to be introduced from the New World in the sixteenth century). More exotic items such as olives and figs will also have been served and both are recorded in the archaeological record from Britain.

Much of what was eaten would be familiar to the modern diner although there were some notable exceptions. South-western Spain was famed across the empire for a number of fish-based sauces known as *garum* or *liquamen*. They were made from the fermentation of the crushed guts of various fish such as mackerel, eel and tuna, and although to our tastes this may not sound especially appetizing, the resulting sauce was said to be subtle and mild in flavour. Large amphorae (storage jars), many holding over 30 litres each, used for the bulk transportation of this and other Mediterranean foodstuffs are common finds on Romano-British sites. All of the courses will have been washed down with wine. Most of the wine consumed was imported from other provinces, although there is some evidence for Roman viticulture from the Welland Valley in Northamptonshire. By the fourth century AD most of the wine drunk in Britain would have come from southern and eastern Gaul (France) and Spain but there is also some evidence for importation from as far afield as North Africa and parts of modern Turkey. Like many of the foodstuffs, much of the wine will have been imported in ceramic amphorae. Each production region manufactured vessels of different and distinctive shapes, which allow archaeologists to identify their source. At Silchester Roman town in Hampshire large wooden barrels were found which had once contained wine. The wood was identified as being Pyrenean pine suggesting that the wine had come from the region of the border between modern France and Spain. Roman wine was quite thick and closer to syrup in consistency than the modern equivalent. This had to be passed through a strainer to remove any impurities and then mixed with water before serving; the preferred ratio being two parts water to one part wine. To drink wine undiluted was considered to be both 'barbarian' and bad mannered.

The food, drink and entertainment served at a great formal banquet will have been viewed by the guests as an adjunct to the rich appointment of the villa and therefore a further reflection of the owners' romanisation, wealth and status.

At the end of the meal the guests would disperse, some perhaps to one of the neighbouring villas known at Colerne or Atworth. More important guests and those from further afield would expect to be given accommodation for the night, possibly in the west range where comfortable suites of rooms are known through excavation.

Away from home the family would have sought entertainment, specialist services and market access to luxury commodities in the local towns such as Bath or Cirencester. Bath perhaps offered a more cosmopolitan sample of the Roman world with a reputation known beyond the boundaries of the province, attracting luxury goods and pilgrims from afar. Being famed as a healing shrine Bath will also have attracted physicians (some perhaps from as far afield as Greece, which was famed for medicinal learning and skills) and no doubt 'quacks' too! Cirencester, as provincial capital in the fourth century, would be a place where business was conducted and political alliances could be formed. The town will have been the main regional financial centre and housed the office of the governor. Also, in its capacity as a local centre, we could anticipate that the owner of Box would be required in the town to sit on the equivalent of a County Council; indeed he may even have owned one of the large and well-appointed urban houses revealed by recent excavations within the town. Cirencester also boasted an amphitheatre and although full blown gladiatorial combats were probably rare, it would have provided access to entertainments and spectacles not otherwise seen in the countryside, including public executions.

Such was the life and daily routine for the villa owner and his family. How the rest of the household lived would have been quite different. A complex on the scale of Box would have required a large number of people to run and maintain it. Some will have been slaves; others employed freedmen and their families. We do not as yet know the location of the quarters for these people but they must have been extensive, as a house on the scale of Box would have required a large workforce. Some, such as personal maids, wet nurses and private secretaries, probably lived in the main house as they would be required at any time. The remainder may have been housed in quarters located in the postulated outer courtyard or in the ranges known to extend into the garden of the Vicarage. Based on comparison with other fully excavated sites these people, who will have formed the majority of the population, may have shared halls used both as accommodation and as a workspace; they will also have had their own bath-suites.

The domestic slaves were seen as an important part of the extended family in the Roman world and should not be seen in the same light as the slaves traded between Africa and North America in the seventeenth and eighteenth centuries. Tombstones erected to slaves and ex-slaves by their owners demonstrate the affection and respect which could exist between the two. There are cases where an ex-slave even married her former owner and after death had a lavish tombstone erected depicting her in the manner of a high ranking Roman lady seated on a wicker chair with a jewellery box at her feet. A fine example is known from the Roman fort at South Shields on Tyneside (Figure 66).

Household slaves and free-born workers could also receive an education and attain a reasonable level of literacy, as many of them would have been destined for administrative jobs either in the villa or in running the estate. Although the lot of the household slave and worker was not as bad as their more recent equivalents, life for them in the fourth century will have contrasted greatly to that of their wealthy owners. Movement between classes became increasingly difficult in the later Roman period with only a military career offering any small hope of improvement, either through merit or intrigue. For most of those who worked the land life, although relatively secure, would have been as routine and monotonous as that of their medieval peasant successors.

If we are correct in our suggestion that the Roman complex at Box also included a major religious focus, we should also reconstruct some of the activities likely to have been practised there.

66 Tombstone of the ex-slave woman Regina found at South Shields. She was married to her former master, a man named Barates, probably a military flag maker who came from the city of Palmyra in modern Syria. Regina was British and probably from somewhere in the area of modern Hertfordshire

Roman religion was complex with literally hundreds of deities to worship. These ranged from the full Roman pantheon such as Jupiter, Juno and Minerva to local spirits protecting a specific location. We have already seen in Chapter Two how the major religious centre at Bath embodied the Roman practice of amalgamating local and Roman deities with the cult of Sulis-Minerva. The depiction of the deities could also vary greatly, ranging from classical images in the Graeco-Roman tradition through to very simple reliefs in a local style but full of vitality (Figure 67).

The evidence from Box is slim but the few religious artefacts recovered do offer some indication of the focus of worship. The fragmentary sculpture of a hand bearing a trident points to a connection with water and a reference to the nearby springs. The votive silver eye points to a healing cult and these were frequently associated with water and springs. The relief depicting a hunter deity would sit comfortably in any rural religious site where the surrounding landscape was rich in game. Few religious sites in Roman Britain

67 Relief from Cirencester showing the 'Genii Cucullatii' or hooded spirits

were dedicated to a single deity and Box appears to be no different.

The layout of the religious site to the west of the villa is poorly understood but there is evidence for heated rooms and drains, these probably being part of a bath-suite; and a long corridor or *porticus* linking it to the villa. It is likely that the level area now occupied by the garden of Box House was enclosed, the boundary being a wall, a ditch or a combination of both and would define a sacred area known as the Temenos. Within the Temenos there would be a number of buildings and large open spaces, some perhaps laid out as formal gardens. The bath-suite was part of a ritual complex where worshippers would bathe and perhaps don special clothing before entering the Temenos. Here there were one or more temples and shrines which were likely to be in an architectural style called 'Romano-Celtic'. This form of building was very different in appearance from the classical style temples that we all associate with Greek and Roman religious buildings, and which had triangular pediments supported on rows of columns. The Romano-Celtic temple was usually square in plan, sometimes circular or multangular, and comprised a central structure often of two or more stories, surrounded by a single storey ambulatory. The origin of this temple plan is pre-Roman and can be traced at least as far back as the third century BC. The type is restricted to north-western Europe and was found across Britain, northern France, Belgium and the Rhineland of Germany.

Worshippers did not enter the temple, this being considered a very sacred space housing the cult object and only to be accessed by the officiating priests. The closest the worshipper could get would be the surrounding ambulatory, where he might perhaps catch a glimpse of a statue of the god through the door of the inner temple. Most worship, sacrifices and the making of offerings would be done outdoors. Many worshippers would bring animals to offer as sacrifices to the gods and these could range from a chicken to a fully grown ox, the choice of beast no doubt in part dictated by financial circumstance. The actual sacrifice was carried out by a priest and had to follow a carefully prescribed sequence to make it acceptable to the gods (Figure 68).

In some cases, following the sacrifice the officiating priest would also practice the ancient art of divination, and read the entrails to foretell the future. Some of the sacrifices would be part of a ritual asking the gods for particular favours while others were in thanks for the fulfilment of a request, and after giving the gods their share by burning it on an altar, the rest of the beast would probably be consumed by the worshippers. Carved stone altars were scattered around the grounds of the Temenos and bore inscriptions giving the name of the god and of the donor. The wealthier worshippers may even have erected statues to offer thanks for favours. Just as at nearby Bath, worshippers might also leave written curses on lead sheets to be directed against those whom they perceived to have wronged them.

68 Roman relief depicting the sacrifice of a pig in front of an altar. The beast has been decked in a garland of flowers and the figure in the centre is pouring a libation on to the altar while the figure on the left holds the sacrificial knife

We may also speculate that if Box was a healing shrine there would have been pools in which the afflicted could bathe. These might be supplemented by special guesthouses where the worshipper and supplicant could spend the night in the hope of seeing the god or goddess in a vision. Buildings possibly fulfilling this purpose have been identified at the rural shrines of Lydney and Uley in Gloucestershire and Nettleton in Wiltshire, the latter only a few miles distant from Box.

Away from the main shrines and temples there would also be further buildings housing shops and stalls selling votive objects and food.

Box in the fourth century AD was an exceptionally wealthy and extensive centre serving many functions. This complex, Romano-British in origin, will have been instantly recognisable to a visitor from another part of the empire as a centre of wealth and power, and of people who saw themselves as Roman.

7
The End of Roman Britain, the Decline of the Villa and After

THE END OF Roman Britain is a subject that continues to excite heated debate among all who are interested in the subject, whether academic or amateur. There are some who believe that the Province was already in a terminal decline before the year 400AD. Others prefer a gradual change, spanning a century or longer, during which Roman institutions fragmented and gave way to new British or Anglo-Saxon kingdoms. The truth probably lies somewhere between these two views and there were clear regional variations. Before reconstructing the fate of the Box villa in the aftermath of Roman rule we need to review what was happening in Britain during the fourth century AD.

In Chapter Five the beginning of the fourth century was introduced as a period of great investment in villas across Roman Britain. The province was secure and the archaeological evidence points to a period of sustained prosperity. This coincides with the establishment of a new dynasty in control of the Roman Empire which was consolidated by the Emperor Constantine I (Figure 69).

Rebels, Rebellion and Barbarians

ELEVATED TO THE throne by the garrison of Britain at the great fortress of York in 306AD, Constantine, after a period of civil war, reunited the empire. He completed reforms of the army and civil service begun by his immediate predecessors and restructured the administration of the Provinces. Britain was reorganised as four separate provinces, each with its own governor and capital. In many respects this reorganisation reflected some of the pre-existing regional groupings which went back to the pre-Roman tribal pattern. The new provinces were centred on London, probably Lincoln, York and Cirencester. Box will now be in the province of Britannia Prima which included most of western Britain (including much of Wales)

69 Bronze coin minted at London 313-314AD showing the portrait of the emperor Constantine I and a depiction of the sun God Sol

and administered from Cirencester. Britannia Prima also appears to have been the wealthiest of the four new provinces, incorporating most of the rich farmland of southern and western Britain, a large number of villas and the mineral wealth of the far west. On his deathbed in 337AD Constantine received

70 Coin of the Emperor Constans depicting the Emperor in a galley holding the labarum, a standard bearing the Christian Chi-Rho monogram

baptism and the empire, now officially Christian, was divided amongst his three surviving sons, Britain coming under the control of Constantine II. Following a dispute in 340AD Constantine II was killed by his brother Constans and the Empire divided into eastern and western parts centred on Constantinople and Rome.

The administrative changes introduced under Constantine and continued by his successors increased levels of state control over most aspects of life. There was also a much greater concentration of wealth into fewer hands and much of the rural population

was now legally tied to the great estate owners. It is clear from the evidence of the villas and rich town houses that the landowning classes in Britannia Prima were flourishing under the new system. Although heavily taxed they were still able to accrue considerable wealth

71 Coin of the usurper Magnentius featuring a prominent Chi-Rho monogram

and live a life of luxury and privilege. Given the sums they contributed to the maintenance of the state, it seems that a number of the wealthy class wanted a greater say in the way the Empire was governed and there is evidence for this mood in Britain. Contemporary accounts tell of the emperor Constans having to come to Britain in the winter of 343AD (Figure 70).

We do not know the details behind this visit but for an emperor to make a hazardous winter crossing of the English Channel would suggest serious unrest. Seven years later, in 350AD, a usurper named Magnentius was declared emperor with the backing of the army in Britain (Figure 71).

Magnentius took troops across the English Channel and killed the legitimate emperor Constans. This rebellion was finally suppressed in 353AD by the surviving son of Constantine I, Constantius II. Here the contemporary accounts are now more informative. We are told that Magnentius had many powerful supporters in Britain and Constantius II sent a trusted henchman, Paul, nicknamed 'The Chain' to punish them. It is recorded that many were executed and their estates were confiscated, and it has been suggested that the decline of a number of villas in the area of modern Hertfordshire may point to the activities of Paul 'The Chain'.

In Britannia Prima there is no discernible change in the fortunes of villas of the Cotswolds and surrounding area, including Box, and it is possible that there was less support for the rebellion here.

The study of fourth-century coin supply patterns to Britain strongly suggests that the Roman state invested heavily in the province of Britannia Prima in the 360s and 370s AD. The archaeological evidence shows no sign of serious decline in the standards of living in the countryside. This is in spite of a contemporary reference to Britain having suffered a serious combined assault from barbarian forces in 367AD, naming the Picts, Saxons, the Attacotti and the Scots (at this time the latter are still based in their original homeland of northern Ireland). This is called the 'Barbarian Conspiracy' and is the first direct reference to the Saxons attacking Britain. The contemporary accounts then continue to tell us that it took almost two years for the situation to be brought under control. Curiously, the archaeological evidence for widespread devastation is absent and it is possible the effects of the raids were quite localised and exaggerated for propaganda purposes. Certainly in Britannia Prima the towns and villas appear to continue without obvious disruption and the recently excavated villas near Box, Atworth and Bradford on Avon, appear to be unscathed at this time. The slight evidence for burning at Box cannot be attributed to any specific event and could easily be the result of an accident rather than enemy action.

A further rebellion raised in Britain during 383AD led to the five-year reign of a usurper named Magnus Maximus. Again it is probable that powerful British interests supported the rebel emperor. Restored to central control in 388AD, Britain continued to be an important part of the western Empire, and between 396 and 398AD it is thought that the most senior Roman commander

72 *A contemporary portrait of the general Stilicho carved in ivory. Although a barbarian of Vandal origin, Stilicho was one of the most able of all late Roman generals.*

in the west, Stilicho, may have campaigned here in AD399 (Figure 72).

The actual end of Roman rule over Britain is difficult to define. The traditional date of 410AD is based on a copy of a letter supposed to have been sent by the emperor Honorius telling the Britons to look to their own defence (Figure 73).

The accuracy of this has been disputed and some now believe that the letter was intended for the people of Bruttium in southern Italy rather than Britannia. We know of a series of final rebellions against central government in Britain during 406AD and 407AD which culminated in the elevation of a man who called himself Constantine III (Figure 74). Constantine III was concerned with securing the Rhine frontier which had suffered numerous barbarian incursions and it is assumed he took troops from Britain to help achieve this. If Britain was to remain part of the Roman world the security of the mainland frontiers in the west was critical. Constantine

73 *A contemporary portrait of the Emperor Honorius carved in ivory and dating to about 406AD.*

74 Gold coin of Constantine III, the last Imperial usurper raised in Britain in 407AD

III was deposed and killed in 411AD and, as the Rhine frontier defences gradually failed, the opportunity to re-establish direct Roman rule diminished and the supply of freshly minted coinage to pay officials and soldiers was reduced to a trickle. The lack of a fresh coinage supply will not have had an immediate effect but eventually the lack of a centralised fiscal authority with sufficient funds will have had an adverse impact on the provincial economy.

It is events during the opening decades of the fifth century AD about which much debate still rages. Ongoing research now suggests that Britain had not been entirely stripped of troops. We now know that a number of forts on Hadrian's Wall and the south coast of Britain were still occupied in the fifth century. There can be no doubt that the majority of the population would still have viewed themselves as part of the Roman world at this date, even if the future was uncertain. The archaeological record also makes it absolutely clear that there were new regional patterns emerging. In the east of the country settlements of Anglo-Saxon character began to appear. In the west, furthest from the North Sea coast facing the Germanic homelands, there is very little evidence for an Anglo-Saxon presence throughout most of the fifth century.

After Roman Britain

IN THE BOX and Bath area evidence for Anglo-Saxon presence does not occur until the sixth century at the earliest, and a prolonged Romanised British survival seems certain. This may at first have encompassed much of the old province of Britannia Prima but then probably broke down into the old tribal units upon which Roman rule had originally been based. We may envisage a series of semi-independent enclaves centred, perhaps, on the larger towns and ruled by the surviving Romano-British aristocracy.

The collapse of Roman rule in the west of the Empire left a power vacuum. In Gaul, modern France, where we have more surviving literary accounts of this period, we know that a number of leading aristocrats sought to maintain their position and status by becoming senior members of the clergy, often as bishops. In the outlying provinces the church will now have become the only widespread surviving institution from the Western Roman Empire. A similar situation is likely in Britain. There are references to a visit by St Germanus, the bishop of Auxerre, to the shrine of St Alban, probably at Verulamium, modern St Albans, in 429AD. He was there at the invitation of local clergy and laity to tackle a heretical movement, the Pelagian heresy, championed by a cleric named Pelagius of British origin. This tantalising glimpse of fifth century Britain shows that there were still people in authority, that there were some surviving urban centres and, despite the collapse of Roman rule, there was still the time and will to engage in debate over doctrinal differences. Little of this smacks of a 'Dark Age' of destruction and desolation.

Whether all villas and landowners survived the collapse of the Roman Empire cannot be known. Some owners, especially those not of British birth, may have moved away to Gaul, including Brittany or even Italy. Some may have lost their estates in local disputes and land grabs while others, possibly the majority, would not have had any alternative but to stay and try to continue with life as best as possible. The collapse of a demanding, centralised economy would eventually have had a profound impact although the increasing lack of coinage will have made surplus produce such as grain important for barter.

In some parts of western Britain a number of pre-Roman hillforts were reoccupied in the sixth century and their defences refurbished. Excavation at a number of these, such as South Cadbury near Ilchester and Cadbury Congresbury near Yatton, have produced pottery imported from the Byzantine Empire (the surviving part of the Roman Empire in the eastern Mediterranean and centred on Constantinople). The pottery includes amphorae (storage jars) which contained wine and olive oil as well as fine red-slipped table wares from North Africa. Where this reoccupation occurred, it may indicate that there was deterioration in security which necessitated the move to a more secure local strongpoint. Whether any of the hillforts in the vicinity of Bath and Box were reoccupied must await further excavation.

Although the archaeological evidence for the early post-Roman period at Box is lacking, much of it probably being removed without record during the original excavations, other sites in the region are very informative. At Bath the precinct of the Temple to Sulis-Minerva appears to have been maintained and there is some pottery and metalwork to indicate continued use of the site (although whether it was still a pagan centre may be in doubt). At other towns further afield such as Wroxeter in Shropshire and Silchester in Hampshire recent excavations have demonstrated that romanised town life survived into the seventh century AD.

In western Britain recent research excavations have produced a growing body of evidence for the survival of a number of villas into the post-Roman period. At Dinnington near Ilminster in Somerset a large and luxuriously appointed villa house seems to have been given over to large-scale grain storage and processing. Rooms which once housed fine mosaics were now either used as granaries or seem to have had more mundane domestic uses with fires being lit directly on the floors. Radio-carbon dates from Dinnington show the villa was still functioning as a farm, and possibly an estate centre given the large storage capacity, into the seventh century AD before being destroyed in a fire. Evidence of continued use of a villa as a farm into the seventh century comes from Frocester Court near Stroud.

Although no record of the post-Roman archaeology survives from Box, the heavily scorched area on the mortar floor and adjacent wall in room 12 could derive from post-Roman use. Close to Box, the villa at Atworth appears to have continued into at least the fifth century, and a number of the grain-drying or malting kilns built inside the main house may belong to this date. The most compelling local evidence for post-Roman villa activity is from Bradford on Avon where a possible Christian baptistery was built in the centre of the main villa house. This certainly dates to the earlier fifth century AD and there is evidence for continued industrial activity elsewhere on the site. The Bradford villa may not have been abandoned until the seventh century AD when the region formally came under the control of the Saxon kingdom of Wessex.

Where the archaeological evidence can be recovered there is a strong impression that villa life in some parts of western Britain may have continued in some form for up to two hundred years before finally being abandoned. The emphasis now appears to be on the production of food rather than the maintenance of grand rooms and a romanised aristocratic lifestyle. The factors governing the abandonment of villas are probably complex and will vary from region to region. At present we can only speculate as to the fate of the owners of Box. To date no artefacts of fifth or sixth century date have been identified there.

How big a factor the Anglo-Saxons played directly in the early post-Roman history of the Box region is debatable. We have already seen that there is little archaeological evidence for their presence in the region before the late-sixth century AD. There is however one literary reference in the great Anglo-Saxon historical source, The Anglo-Saxon Chronicle, which must be discussed. The Anglo-Saxon Chronicle survives in a number of editions and originated as an oral tradition mixing a collection of myths and historical events. These were finally written down, in English, from the ninth century onwards. The entry for the year 577 reads 'Now Cuthwine and Ceawline fought with the Britons, and three kings they slew, Commagil, Condidan, and Farinmagil in the place that is called Deorham and they took three cities, Glevan-ceaster, Ciren-ceaster and Bathan-Ceaster'. Ceawlin was king of the West Saxons and Cuthwine his son. The place named as Deorham is generally accepted to be modern Dyrham, north of Bath and just off the modern A46. The three cities reported as captured are clearly Gloucester, Cirencester and Bath, the major Roman towns of the region. Here we are apparently told in no uncertain terms that the Britons suffered a major military defeat and that territory was lost. Curiously, the archaeological evidence to support this claim is lacking or yet to be recognised. What is of interest are the names of the three defeated British kings; these are thought to be, at least in part, of Irish origin. The role of Irish immigrants in the post-Roman period is not yet fully understood but there was considerable movement across the Irish Sea at this time, first as raiders and later as settlers and Christian missionaries. We should remember here that tradition states St Patrick was a young Romano-British nobleman, probably from western Britain – maybe modern Somerset – who was kidnapped from his father's estate by Irish raiders in the late fourth century.

75 *The church of St Thomas Becket, Box. The present building dates from the thirteenth century and sits over part of the villa west range*

There is a further feature of the Box villa which needs to be discussed in connection with the post-Roman history of the site. Part of the villa is today occupied by the medieval church of St Thomas Becket (Figure 75).

There is frequently an association between medieval churches and Roman buildings, although the reason for this is not always obvious. In some cases it may simply be that the Roman ruins have provided a shell suitable for modification or as a convenient source of building materials. This is almost certainly the case in Leicester where the Anglo-Saxon church of St Nicholas reused part of the Roman public baths. Closer to Box, Bath Abbey, an Anglo-Saxon foundation, stands close to the Roman temple precinct, the main bathing establishment, and may occupy the site of another Roman religious monument. In this case it is very tempting to see the siting of the abbey church as a deliberate act to claim the former pagan centre for Christianity.

In central Wiltshire the Medieval parish churches of Cherhill and Manningford Bruce are known to occupy parts of very large villas with others suspected at Amesbury and Britford near Salisbury (the latter two churches of proven Anglo-Saxon origin). The present church at Box dates mainly from the thirteenth century and later, although an Anglo-Saxon origin is possible given an association with St Aldhelm. Aldhelm was an early eighth century monk of Malmesbury Abbey who became Bishop of Sherborne, and is traditionally associated with the origins of stone quarrying at Hazelbury. The significance of the coincidence of a Roman villa and a Medieval church is unclear. Some have been tempted to suggest that the presence of a church on a villa site may be evidence for the continuation of a late Roman house church. Such cases are better documented in France but have yet to be proven in Britain. Without extensive excavation below the church, along with all the disruption this would create and no guarantee of any surviving remains, it is impossible to arrive at any firm view.

After the final abandonment of the villa, possibly in the seventh century based on the evidence from other sites, the building will have begun to decay. Once the roof had collapsed the structure would have been open to the elements, wall plaster will have crumbled, frost will have damaged the mortar and stonework loosened. The site may then have lain derelict for some considerable time and the great audience chamber, room 26, would no doubt have been a particularly impressive ruin. At this point it is worth quoting part of an incomplete eighth-century AD Anglo-Saxon poem called 'The Ruin' and written in Old English. The poem is actually thought to be a description of the Roman baths in Bath:

> This masonry is wondrous; fates broke it courtyard pavements were smashed; the work of giants is decaying. Roofs are fallen, ruinous towers, the frosty gate with frost on cement is ravaged, chipped roofs are torn, fallen, undermined by old age. The grasp of the earth possesses the mighty builders, perished and fallen, the hard grasp of earth, until a hundred generations of

people have departed . . . Bright were the castle buildings, many the bathing-halls, high the abundance of gables, great the noise of the multitude, many a meadhall full of festivity, until Fate the mighty changed that. Far and wide the slain perished, days of pestilence came, death took all the brave men away; their places of war became deserted places, the city decayed. The rebuilders perished, the armies to earth. And so these buildings grow desolate, and this red-curved roof parts from its tiles of the ceiling-vault. The ruin has fallen to the ground broken into mounds . . .

This is just an extract from the work but gives a wonderful contemporary eye-witness account of a massive Roman building in decay.

The ruins of the villa were probably visible for some considerable time, there being little new building in stone, apart from churches and castles, between the end of the Roman period and the high Middle Ages. The 1967 excavation did find evidence for the deliberate demolition of the walls of the villa and some of the robbing trenches contained medieval pottery of twelfth to thirteenth century date. This is the period when many Roman buildings disappeared from view and there may be correlation with an increase in the construction of domestic stone buildings from the thirteenth century onwards. A ruin on the scale of the Box villa would have been an ideal source of dressed building stone and limestone to burn for the manufacturing of lime mortar and plaster.

Although Box is not mentioned in the Domesday Book compiled in 1086, it is probable that a settlement did exist here at the time of the Norman conquest. The Domesday Book mentions Ditteridge and Hazelbury, recording two mills at the latter. The mills must have been some distance from Hazelbury given its hilltop location, and these were most likely adjacent to the By Brook in or near Box. The ever reliable springs around Box church would have had the same attraction for settlement as they did to the prehistoric and Roman populations.

By the later medieval period part of the villa site had been built over and the parish church was over the southern end of the west range. A water-mill is known, possibly one of those mentioned in the Domesday Book, and stood on the site of The Wilderness. The pond in the grounds of The Wilderness is a remnant of the original mill-pond. Walling from the levelled remains of the mill was noted by Sir Harold Brakspear in his account of the excavation of the west range of the villa although no plan of the remains was made.

The memory of a large Roman building at Box was probably never forgotten locally. Constant use of the churchyard during the medieval period must have exposed Roman remains during the digging of graves and the later anecdotal accounts of mosaics found by the church probably reflect this.

Apart from a short stretch of wall in the garden of The Wilderness and a few courses of wall to the west of the church, there is nothing visible above ground of this once magnificent building. Despite the extensive excavations during the nineteenth century there is still much to be learned about the Box Roman villa. The potential of the site as an important archaeological resource has yet to be realised and the full extent of the site still to be determined and this, at least, must be a priority for future investigation.

Thoughts for the direction of further investigations are given in the next chapter.

8
The Future of the Villa

THE ROMAN VILLA at Box has been known for almost two hundred years and the main ranges have been excavated on a number of occasions over this period. The motivation for excavation has ranged from antiquarian curiosity and commercial exploitation to meticulous modern archaeological investigation. The cumulative results of this work have produced an as yet incomplete plan of one of the largest Roman villas in south-west Britain with evidence for at least twenty mosaic floors. Despite the lengthy period of investigation there is still much to learn. The Roman ditch in the grounds of The Hermitage excavated by Mrs Carless in 1982 which produced large quantities of building debris and second century AD pottery suggests that further structures await discovery well beyond the known limits of the site.

Questions

THERE ARE A great many questions still to be answered and the full extent of the site remains unknown. The southern limit of the main house has yet to be determined and the structures discovered in the grounds of The Vicarage and Box House still need to be fully identified and characterised. The latter area is unusual in form and difficult to parallel on other Romano-British villas. The presence of springs, fragments of sculpture and possible votive objects all suggest a religious function and the strong possibility of a shrine adjacent to the villa needs to be investigated further. Apart from the pottery recovered from the ditch in The Hermitage garden, the site has produced very little pottery, coins or other artefacts. This suggests that the area of the villa house was kept clean throughout the period of occupation and that rubbish was dumped elsewhere; there must be middens nearby. The location and investigation of these would provide dateable material allowing a more detailed chronology to be established. If we are correct in interpreting the villa as a great estate centre, the normal range of agricultural buildings and accommodation for the household and estate workers still await discovery.

76 Plan of the villa complex and the boundary of the Scheduled Ancient Monument

The core of the known complex is today protected as a Scheduled Ancient Monument; this encompasses an area of just over 1 hectare (2½ acres) and includes all of the grounds of The Wilderness, The Vicarage, Roman Villas, Box House Cottage and part of the grounds of Box House. The churchyard, The Hermitage and the southern part of the grounds of Box House are currently excluded from the scheduled area. Although it does not include all of the potential area of Roman archaeology, the scheduled status acknowledges the national importance of the site and it gives legal protection from unauthorised development and excavation. Any disturbance to the ground within this boundary, including archaeological investigation, can only be undertaken with the written consent of the Minister of State for Culture, Media and Sport as advised by the English Heritage Inspector of Ancient Monuments. The plan of the designated Scheduled Ancient Monument (Figure 76) makes it clear that the Roman site must extend beyond the current boundary of the scheduled area.

Despite the presence of so many later structures the site still has considerable archaeological potential. The 1967 re-excavation of room 26 in the north-east corner of demonstrated the survival of extensive undisturbed archaeological deposits despite the earlier investigations. This is especially important for the remains of the earlier villa and it is clear that most of the nineteenth and early twentieth century works only exposed the uppermost, late Roman levels. The excavations in the grounds of Box House, Box House Cottage, The Wilderness and The Vicarage have established the presence of well-preserved remains in these locations, each with a considerable depth of surviving archaeological deposits.

Future Work

THE PRIORITY FOR future research must be to establish the full extent of the Roman building complex. Further large-scale excavation is unlikely in the near future. If this was proposed within the protected area Scheduled Monument Consent would be required and significant funding sought; archaeological research projects are very expensive. Modern excavation requires a range of disciplines with the participation of many specialists to compile reports and prepare the results for publication. Financial provision for the long term conservation and storage of the excavation archive is also required.

At present any building or ground works in the immediate vicinity of the villa has to be subject to a planning constraint requiring the presence of a qualified archaeologist to monitor and observe the operations. Given the potential of the site this stipulation should ideally be extended to cover a larger area of the village in the hope of encountering and recording further significant archaeological deposits. This is especially so for areas to the south and west of the known remains.

Archaeology is often viewed purely as excavation but this is itself a destructive process and is only one of a number of investigative methods now available. Current archaeological philosophy recognises that any buried remains represent a finite resource and that excavation should only be undertaken after all available non-intrusive methods have been applied, or there is an unavoidable threat of serious damage or destruction. At Box the presence of numerous modern structures over part of the Roman remains is a challenge to further investigation.

A widely used tool in modern archaeology is geophysics. This technique is now familiar to millions after prolonged use on popular television archaeology programmes such as 'Time Team'. The term incorporates a number of non-intrusive methods used to scan for buried features such as ditches, pits and walls.

Gradiometry, also often referred to as magnetometry, will detect soils and deposits with an enhanced magnetic signature as a result of burning and general human activity. The method is especially good for detecting buried pits and ditches but will also, on occasion, give the outline of buried walls. This method was used with great effect during the initial investigations at St Laurence School, Bradford on Avon and revealed a detailed plan of numerous Roman buildings and other features (Figure 77).

For locating buried walls and compact surfaces a method called electrical resistance survey can be used. This measures resistance to an electric current passed between two probes.

Where the geological conditions are suitable the application of both methods can produce remarkably detailed results. Theoretically the limestone geology of the Box area should be suitable for the application of these methods although local factors such as the depth of soil overburden can significantly affect results.

Limited gradiometry and electrical resistance surveys have already been undertaken in the grounds of The Wilderness but with mediocre success. One of the surveys was undertaken during damp weather and this may have had an adverse effect on the results. The increasing sensitivity of the geophysical equipment now available, coupled with the latest data processing software, makes this the most attractive and cost effective

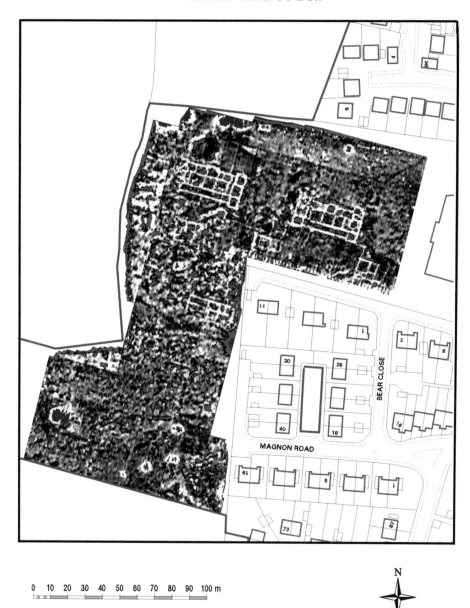

0 10 20 30 40 50 60 70 80 90 100 m

N

77 Plan of the Roman villa at St Laurence School, Bradford on Avon as revealed by gradiometer survey. The white lines mark the position of buried walls

method of investigation. The method has much to commend it, not least the fact that it causes no disturbance of the buried archaeology.

There is potential for geophysical investigation in a number of areas over the villa and its immediate environs. The grounds of Box House, The

Wilderness, The Vicarage and the properties to the rear of Valens Terrace would undoubtedly make prime targets for geophysical survey. The area of the Bowling Green and open ground to the east of the villa, although heavily landscaped, would also be suitable for geophysical survey to ascertain whether localised archaeological deposits still survive here.

The churchyard is a critical area for establishing the full extent of the west range of the villa (and it should be recalled here that a short length of Roman wall is still extant to the west of the church). Antiquarian accounts record that remains have been found here, including mosaics, presumably encountered during the digging of graves. Archaeological excavation in the churchyard is clearly not possible and gradiometry or electrical resistance survey is unlikely to produce coherent results in ground which has been subjected to prolonged disturbance from grave digging. Despite this another technique, Ground Penetrating Radar (GPR), may bear results. This is a relatively new method in archaeology which allows a deeper penetration of the subsoil and, unlike the other geophysical methods described, can 'see' through solid surfaces such as stone slabs and tarmac. GPR also allows an image to be produced for a specific depth, called a 'time slice', and this capability makes it a potential tool for use in an area like a churchyard. It should theoretically be possible to 'see' any buried archaeological remains which may survive below the level of disturbance caused by the excavation of graves. The method has recently been used with some success in locating the remains of an exceptionally large Roman building known to extend into the medieval churchyard of the village of Castor near Peterborough.

More practical and 'hands on' methods can be employed which are suitable for widespread participation as a community archaeology project conducted under professional archaeological guidance.

Where geophysics is not possible, whether due to thick vegetation or only a small area of ground being available, a series of small scale trial excavations can be undertaken. This can take the form of hand-dug test pits, one metre square and excavated to a depth where undisturbed archaeological deposits are encountered. This method is fast, requires little capital outlay and if the location of the pits is carefully planned can rapidly establish the extent of undisturbed archaeological remains.

Where the digging of pits may be considered undesirable or impractical, a survey of local gardens to record any artefacts and building materials exposed on the surface in flower beds and vegetable plots may give an approximate indication of the extent of archaeological deposits. This method allows participation of all age groups and properly coordinated can provide a great deal of useful information. At St Laurence School, Bradford on Avon, a garden survey of the housing estate adjacent to the site proved very successful in identifying a further 2 hectares (5 acres) of potential Roman settlement.

Looking beyond the immediate environs of the villa at Box there is scope for a series of further investigations focusing on the Roman landscape setting. The main source for this is the large collection of aerial photographs held by English Heritage and Wiltshire Council which can be used to plot plough-levelled archaeological features and surviving earthworks. Using this method it should be possible partially to reconstruct field patterns, seek for evidence of the local Roman road network and identify further settlements.

The complex at Box is one of the most important rural Roman sites in western Roman Britain and deserves to be more widely known. The evidence for the extent and nature of the site and its setting has been analysed and a reconstruction of Romano-British villa life presented. There is still much to learn about this fascinating site and despite the practical difficulties presented by a site which has extensive modern overburden, ways of continuing investigations are suggested. It is hoped that this account will have intrigued the reader and will stimulate interest in further investigations by future generations of professional and amateur archaeologists.

It is hoped that this book has explained the contribution and the potential of the Romano-British structures at Box. The site demonstrates the remarkable changes our ancestors experienced when Rome added Britain to her empire, building roads, developing towns and above all teaching the Britons how to *live the Roman way.*

The building techniques, crafts, administration and culture were all Roman, but the people who practiced them were largely Britons plus merchants and ex-soldiers from other parts of the Roman Empire. There were certainly other parts of the Roman Empire that inherited the advantages of Roman tradition in perhaps greater measure than Britain but in the southern part of the country, where the Box villa was situated, Romanisation had perhaps reached its highest level.

It is a sobering thought to realise that here in Box some 1,600 years ago there lived a sophisticated community, the upper classes of which had every material comfort. They had window glass, central heating, beautiful interior decoration, sophisticated cuisine, imported fine wines and well tailored clothes.

We can perhaps learn much from examination of this age of cultured living exemplified by the Roman complex here in Box, which started almost two thousand years ago and endured for the next four or five hundred years.

Select Bibliography

Note: *WAM = Wiltshire Archaeological and Natural History Magazine*

Aubrey, J. 1982, *Monumenta Britannica: a Miscellany of British Antiquities.* (Edited by
J. Fowles)

Bescoby, D. 2008, Box Roman Villa: a preliminary geophysical investigation.
Unpublished ms, University of East Anglia

Brakspear, H. 1904, The Roman Villa at Box. *WAM* 33, 236-69

Carless, K. nd , Draft Archaeology Report on The Hermitage, Box. Unpublished ms,
Wiltshire & Swindon History Centre and Devizes Museum

Corney, M. 2003a, *The Roman Villa at Bradford on Avon: The Investigations of 2002*

Corney, M. 2003b, *The Roman Villa at Bradford on Avon: The Investigations of 2003*

Cosh, S. and Neal, D. 2005, *Roman Mosaics of Britain, Volume II, South-West Britain*

Cunliffe, B.W. 1995, *Roman Bath*

Cunliffe, B.W. and Fulford, M.G. 1982, *Corpus Signorum Imperii Romani: Corpus of
Sculpture in the Roman World. Great Britain. Volume 1 Fascicule 2. Bath and the Rest
of Wessex*

Erskine, J.G.P. and Ellis, P. 2008, Excavations at Atworth Roman Villa, Wiltshire
1970-1975. *WAM* 101, 51-129

Hurst, H. et al, 1987, Excavations at Box Roman Villa 1967-8. *WAM* 81, 19-51

Luckett, L. et al, 2000, Investigation of a Roman villa site at Euridge Manor Farm,
Colerne. *WAM* 93, 218-232

Mann, R. 1887, The Roman Villa at Box. *Journal of the British Archaeological
Association*, 43, 47-55

Mellor, A. Shaw and Goodchild, R.G. 1942, The Roman Villa at Atworth. *WAM* 49,
46-95.

Neal, D. 1974, *The Excavation of the Roman Villa, Gadebridge Park, Hemel Hempstead,
1963-8.* Soc. of Ants. Res. Rept. No XXXI

Smith, J. T. 1996, *Roman Villas, A Study in Social Structure*

White, R. 2007, *Britannia Prima: Britain's Last Roman Province*

Williams, R. and Zeepvat, R. 1994, *Bancroft: A Late Bronze Age/Iron Age Settlement,
Roman Villa and Temple/Mausoleum*

Index of People and Places

Minor places are in Gloucestershire, Somerset or Wiltshire unless otherwise stated